High Praise for *Inside Job*

"This is not a self-help book, but rather a self-fulfillment one. The title's promise is real—between these pages you will find out how to build your work life from the inside out and thrive as a result."
MJ Ryan, author of *This Year I Will:*
How to Finally Change a Habit, Keep a Resolution or
Make a Dream Come True

"Not many people think of freedom as they create their future story on careers. Normally the comments I hear are about what they "have" to do or "the only way to do it is ..." This book offers the freedom of creating and innovating from any starting point. I sure wish I had read it when I was 25."
Debora McDermed-Peila, PhD

"Finally! A career development book that gets it right. Inside Job shows us how to look within to our own innate wisdom and capacities to create our ideal career. I love that the book helps us let go of limiting thoughts like fear and self doubt to discover our resiliency that enables us to live our dream job. This book is truly transformational."
Mark Howard, PhD, Three Principles Institute

Inside Job

8 Secrets to
Loving Your Work and Thriving

Julie Gleeson and Sherry Platt Berman, MA

Inside Job

8 Secrets to Loving Your Work and Thriving

Julie Gleeson and Sherry Platt Berman, MA

Bush Street Press

Copyright © 2012 by Julie Gleeson and Sherry Platt Berman MA

ISBN Print: 978-1-937445-34-8
ISBN Digital/epub: 978-1-937445-35-5
Library of Congress Control Number 2012938909

Dedication

Julie:

Sydney Banks inspired the understanding that made all the work worth writing about.

Debora McDermed-Peila taught me friendship, kindness, love, and forgiveness.

Tim Gleeson, my dear husband, who has faith in me when I do not.

Jane and Don Houser, my parents, who patiently put up with my searching and questioning.

Karen Houser, my twin, without whom I might not know about connection at all.

Diane Houser Evans, who just fulfills her life with no fanfare.

Sherry Platt Berman, who became my extraordinary business partner when I wasn't looking.

All the past and future clients of Career Wisdom Institute, Inc., and The Art of Living, Inc., who are generous of spirit, insight, and heart and the best hires in the world!

And finally, my Norfolk Terriers, who teach me daily about fulfilling life every single moment. In their world, if it isn't fun, it doesn't exist.

Sherry:

For Sam and Elijah who opened my heart to true love and the deep understanding that I have no control in life, only in how I choose to respond. To my brother, Ron, who has always been my devoted and accepting family. To Tzipora and Susan for their deep friendship and support.

For P.E.B., who loved and believed in me utterly and completely, taught me the meaning of intimacy, and introduced me to my beloved Guru.

To Laura, who brought joy, light, and song back into my life.

To Illana Berger, my teacher and mentor, for lifting the veil and deepening the quest.

To The Rainbow Community Center for giving me a place to be out and open and for helping the LGBTQ teens in our community to love themselves.

To Gurumayi whose protection is always behind me.

To Julie Gleeson, for teaching me that a healthy, prosperous business partnership is truly possible.

From Julie and Sherry:

A big thank you to Alicia Dunams, who gave us the structure and guidance we needed to write this book.

Inside Job: 8 Secrets to Loving Your Work and Thriving is dedicated to anyone who believes you cannot love your work and thrive. May the pages in this book remind you that your work is to care for yourself and others by following the dreams you came into this life to fulfill.

Introduction

"Sometimes, people ask, 'Do you think I'll make it?'
Have faith in yourself. Yes, you will make it. Why shouldn't you make
it? Did someone sign a certificate saying you will never make it?
Surely, you can make it.
One of the things to remember is if God has given birth to you,
then that is a sure sign you can make it. He has sent you to this world
with so much faith. So, if you can have even a little bit of that faith,
you will reach the goal."
Swami Chidvilasananda

Staying employed these days is an Inside Job.

What does that mean?

It means that you are the sole creator of your professional work-life experience.

It means knowing and understanding what is unique about you—your given gift—and taking that out into the world. This is your job and will keep you employed and resilient in any circumstances.

An Inside Job means that you no longer rely on the bankrupt industrial revolution and you join the entrepreneurial age. This doesn't necessarily mean working for yourself. It does mean that you go to work from a new, creative perspective.

An Inside Job means never looking online for a job again. You can research companies and potential clients online for information, but stay away from job boards and classified ads. When you work from the inside out, you are led to countless opportunities. You follow the excitement that builds when you see something that aligns with who you are and pursue that like a bloodhound looking for a lost child.

Inside Job means there is no limit to the abundance available because you love what you do. There is a belief in our culture called the work ethic, which teaches us that it is okay to suffer through what we are doing 40 hours a week, 52 weeks a year. The irony of this belief is that you actually limit yourself and the amount of money you make if you dislike your work. It's criminal to put your soul, spirit, and body through something that painful every day and think it is okay. That's like living in an abusive relationship and thinking that's the way love is supposed to feel. When you work from the inside out, there is no limit to how much money you can make because you are doing what you were born to do. You have been given everything you need to be successful. You just need to access what you already possess. The Career Wisdom Institute, Inc. and this book present a new model for career development and success, one that is dedicated to you finding work that is inspired from the inside out.

This is the age of self-determination, and the only job you will ever need is the Inside Job, living your design, and loving your work.

Preface

While perusing career books at a local photocopy store, we noticed that each book provided tips to the reader on how to find work, how to keep from getting fired, and how to stay employed. These books are filled with advice that sell to your fears and provide you with solutions, which is an "outside in" approach to career planning.

Inside Job is not that kind of book.

We are not interested in providing you with quick fixes or small bandages in a feeble attempt to cover large gaping wounds. Our goal is very different. We want to revolutionize the way you *think, feel,* and *experience* work, enhancing your resiliency and employability for the rest of your life. We want to help you to know yourself so well that you will no longer identify with a job title or live inside a box that does not fit.

To do this, we are going to challenge your current notions about work. We are going to shake up your model of career planning; we are going to do our best to put you back in the driver seat of your career.

This is not a "how-to," quick-fix book. There is no such thing when it comes to planning something as important as your career. This book is designed to help you become aware of the things that are stopping you from enjoying your work and your life. This awareness-based teaching will help you to naturally and innately correct your life when it is off track. The 8 Secrets are designed for you to move from being blind and innocently unaware to being wise and able to see. This is how you learn to love your work and thrive!

If you are desperately trying to find work as quickly as you can, Inside Job can help calm you down so you can focus and run a more efficient job search. In our Master Series (and our next book) offered at the Career Wisdom Institute (CWI), we teach you a step-by-step process that has helped so many find work they love and the abundance they deserve.

Those who read and are exposed to the Inside Job: 8 Secrets to Loving your Work and Thriving feel better and are more optimistic about life and their careers. We want you to have fun, relax, and enjoy the journey of loving your life and work. Let it sink in!

Get interested and, for goodness sake, don't believe everything you think.

Table of Contents

"A master in the art of living draws no sharp distinction between his work and his play; his labor and his leisure; his mind and his body; his education and his recreation. He hardly knows which is which. He simply pursues his vision of excellence through whatever he is doing, and leaves others to determine whether he is working or playing. To himself, he always appears to be doing both."

— L.P. Jack from his *Education Through Recreation,*
published in 1932

SECRET #1

Everything You Know About Career Planning is Backward

"I therefore claim to show, not how men think in myths, but how myths operate in men's minds without their being aware of the fact."
Claude Levi Strauss (French Philosopher, 1908)

Joan is a 59-year-old MBA, CPA, and CFO with over 25 years experience managing, directing, and organizing companies around their finances. She has worked for leading consulting firms and is actively recruited for her skills. She has never had difficulty finding a job, comes with superb references, and has an excellent reputation. Yet, with this beautiful professional portfolio and a successful track record, Joan won't make the move to follow her dream and start her own consulting business. Why? Myths!

The myth that ...

◊ *She's not qualified to start her own financial consulting business;*

◊ *No one will want to hire her because she's "too old;"*

◊ *She'll have to work long, hard hours for no pay;*

◊ *There's no opportunity;*

◊   *She'll hate her bosses and work in environments that suck her soul dry;*

◊   *Ultimately, she will end up living in a box under a freeway.*

Joan is also a fierce and adventuresome spirit, whether she's two-stepping at a Western bar, riding white water rapids, surfing in Hawaii, cruising around the world, or driving a motor home by herself up and down the coast of California. She has loved and lost two men to cancer; raised a legally blind son as a single mother while working full time and going to college to get her MBA. Her story is the stuff legends are made of, yet Joan thinks she is afraid of risk. Why? More Myths.

The myth that she:

◊   *Makes poor decisions*

◊   *Is not strong enough*

◊   *Is afraid to try new things*

◊   *Will have to "endure" or "suffer"*

◊   *Can't make decisions*

◊   *Has no choice*

None of these myths are true, but they are powerful. Until Joan learned to think of her life as an Inside Job, they kept her imprisoned in a cycle of unhappiness and scarcity. She knew she needed guidance and support to make a career transition, which is why she came to the Career Wisdom Institute (CWI).

At CWI, we taught Joan how her thinking and her moods might be keeping her stuck in an unsatisfying cycle. We taught her that her career decisions were formed by deep habituated neural pathways in her brain that are unconsciously running her life. She learned about the principles for living, the mood platform, and how to aim for the experience she most wants in life. We also began to uncover her Career Design, which is centered on providing organization for adventuresome projects, people, and events. As an adventurer and businesswoman, this made perfect sense. Now, slowly but surely, Joan is turning her life around and heading toward the life she wants. She is working with small adventure-oriented businesses that are just starting. Joan is their mentor and guide. She is now a well-paid financial consultant to CEOs of the companies that once hired her and kept her in the back room. Most importantly, she is happy because she now has an Inside Job and understands that she can love her work and thrive in any economy. She is free! And you can be, as well.

What if everything you've been told about career planning was a lie? Career Myths told to us by our parents, institutions, cultures, folklore, and historical dogma (work ethic)–include the stories we've made up in our own minds that are false and have no validity, yet are incredibly powerful because they formulate our belief systems about work. When we're doing satisfying work, our work is healing and we are healed through our work. If work is healing, why are so many of us sick about work? Our first Secret brings to light the truths about work.

Myths are traditional or legendary stories passed down in lineage and through cultures. Career myths are often based on the stories created by our ancestors, parents, and/or grandparents, who were raised in a time of scarcity and deprivation and did have to labor at work they didn't love. They were children (or grandchildren) of the Depression, the Holocaust, refugees from war, poverty, scarcity, and fear, deeply entrenched in a belief system that was often punitive and distrustful of money and wealth in general. As children of these children, we've carried this work paradigm into the present time, when, in fact, our reality is very different. Thanks to our parents and theirs, as well, we now have the ability and space to explore satisfaction, abundance, and joy in our work. But we still have these myths deeply embedded into our consciousness and don't take the time to question their validity. We continue to use these myths as our foundation for seeking employment and work, and it's making us miserable.

Here are some of the strongest career myths in our culture today:

◊   You can't make money doing the thing you love;

◊   Career assessments determine the right job for you;

◊   There are "good" careers and "bad" careers;

◊   You need employers more than they need you;

◊   The harder you work, the more money you make;

◊   Goal-setting is the key to success;

◊   You must have a college degree;

◊   You can't find a job in this recession;

◊   Follow the trends, pick the right industries;

◊   Find stable industries like the state and federal government or a big corporation for lifelong employment;

◊   Success means working very hard, very fast, and multitasking;

◊   Art, music, and writing have no value but make great hobbies.

Do any of these sound familiar?

None of these beliefs are true. In fact, they are downright dangerous because they get in the way of creating the right career for yourself. However, you're not alone in believing these myths. We read such ideas and others like them every day in career advice columns and websites and hear them from the pulpit and on television. As the industrial age economy changes and the age of entrepreneurism, village economy, and globalization change the way we've worked for the past 200-plus years, people are uncertain and afraid, making these myths appear even stronger.

Still, they're lies. As conscious career counselors, the two of us are always amazed and saddened by how many people believe, quite strongly, the myth that you have to tolerate being miserable to make a lot of money. The truth is that it is exactly the people who love what they do who find themselves abundant beyond belief. If you work full-time between the ages of 21-65, that's 96,000 hours of pressed, unhappy energy flowing through your system just so you can make a lot of money, which is ultimately impossible because clients don't want to buy from unpleasant people. Co-workers don't want to cooperate with and employers don't want to employ or promote unhappy, unmotivated people who don't like what they are doing. Suffering is the decision not to move beyond your place of miserable comfort, inhibiting your abilities to be creative, accomplished, productive, and make a lot of money!!

According to research conducted at the University of California Riverside, led by Professor Sonja Lyubomirsky, the happier we are, the more likely it is we will have a higher income. Cheerful people are more likely to try new things and challenge themselves, which leads to greater success in work (as well as better relationships and health, by the way). *"There was [also] strong evidence that happiness leads people to be more sociable and more generous, more productive at work, to make more money, and to have stronger immune system*s," said Professor Lyubomirsky.

The business world is constantly researching the effects of being happy and positive in the workplace. The Gallup organization, a performance management consulting company, has spent decades looking at what creates greater productivity and profitability in organizations. The answer in a nutshell? Employee engagement. According to Scarlett Surveys, a company that conducts employee engagement surveys, *"Employee*

Engagement is a measurable degree of an employee's positive or negative emotional attachment to their job, colleagues, and organization which profoundly influences their willingness to learn and perform at work."

If you're not happy at work, you are not only making yourself miserable, but damaging your organization's profitability and your co-workers productivity. *"Actively disengaged employees erode an organization's bottom line while breaking the spirits of colleagues in the process. Within the U.S. workforce, Gallup estimates this cost to be more than $300 billion in lost productivity alone."*

A career myth taught to us from an early age is that there are "good" careers and "bad" careers. The good ones are stable and make a fair income. The bad ones don't provide either. We're taught to squeeze ourselves into a profession without much consideration to who we are and how we want our life to look and feel because it's a secure profession. As a result, we often have a very hard time figuring out what we want to do for work and can end up spending decades unhappily doing something because, "my guidance counselor in high school told me it would be a good career," as one unhappy middle-aged architect told a friend of ours.

Let's look at what these myths have done to the creatives of this world. Most artists believe that their work and contributions have no value. At the Career Wisdom Institute, we hear countless stories from musicians, artists, and writers who were told by their families that their skills were hobbies and had no value in the world. Think of the beauty and imaginative new concepts our culture has lost because of this myth. Luckily, this trend is changing, and we have the Internet to thank for this shift in acceptance of artisans. Companies like Google and Apple rely heavily on their creative people. Music scholarships to major universities are on the rise. Publishers used to have control over the books you read, but now anyone can publish an eBook, make their music available on iTunes, or create movies for YouTube. The possibilities are endless, once you get over the myths.

The myths around what work is suppose to be and how we are expected to approach it are particularly devastating. When we ask people how they define "work," more often than not clients tell us that work is "hard," "suffocating," "stressful," or "a necessary evil"—all thoughts that have been built on the brick and mortar of the career myths. So often, work is seen as a *worthiness* project, this disavowed thing we do to earn something—respect, money, self-worth. Work is treated like the aunt no one really likes who keeps coming over to visit and we can't wait for her to leave so we can go enjoy the rest of our lives. As co-founders of the Career Wisdom Institute, we see it as our job to revolutionize the way you think, feel, and experience work—to change the concept of work from something you do to earn something to being something you do because you can't help doing that thing. Work becomes an extension of who you are, how you heal, how you love, and how you care-er through this world. Is it any wonder that the first four letters of the word career are CARE?

We believe that everyone comes into this life with work they're supposed to accomplish. This is often referred to as a *calling or the soul's great project.* We call it Career Design. Think of life as a puzzle, with each person having a piece of the puzzle that is essential to form a complete picture. If you don't show up with your piece, life isn't whole. Your Career Design reflects the unique configuration of gifts and talents that you have to offer to the world. Work is nothing more than how you decide to focus your energy and bring those special gifts of yours into your life. You embody the gift. You transform the gift; it is your job to bring the gift into the world in its various forms, shapes, and sizes. This is your *work.*

Once you discover your Career Design, the thing that you do that you can't help but do, then you pick your career, create your resume, plan your job search, and prepare for interviews. Your Career Design becomes the foundation on which to make all your career choices (more on this in Secret 8).

This is a powerful shift, because instead of identifying yourself in terms of your job/career, which very likely will change over time, you identify with your gifts and all the different ways they can be used. When you commit to following this Inside Job approach, all the myths will fall away and you will remain employable and resilient in the ever-changing and unpredictable economy. Industries and professions will come and go, but your Design is with you all of your life. When you embrace the truth of whom you are and how you show up in the world, you remain abundant, no matter what.

SECRET #2

Remodeling Your Career

*"People often complain about lack of time when the
lack of direction is the real problem."*
Zig Ziglar

Tam is a lovely, artistic, and insightful woman who came to us with very little fanfare and a lot of frustration. After 15 years experience as a successful marketing director, she found herself spinning in a career that did not feel satisfying or purposeful. She tried several times to leave her profession but was frequently enticed back by recruiters and companies who were offering her jobs that were hard to turn down. Finally, after years of unhappiness, Tam found herself once again frustrated and determined to make a change. *"Though I was an accomplished marketing professional and very much in demand, I knew there was something bigger out there that more aligned with my passions. The heartbreaking thing for me was that, after all this time, I still didn't know which direction to head to find that perfect job."*

Everything you've learned about career planning is backward. It's true! We are told to pick the ideal job and then squeeze ourselves into a box or paradigm that will financially sustain us and keep us employed for a lifetime, even if the job is not aligned with who we are. That's like buying a new pair of shoes because they are a name brand, very shiny and stylish, and incredibly expensive. Then you take the shoes home, walk around, and find they are horribly uncomfortable. They pinch your feet, are way too narrow, and you're hobbling around on the heel. Still you invested so much in these shoes that you feel compelled to wear them. That's often what a job feels like when you choose it from appearances or from the outside in.

The Career Wisdom Institute has created a more effective model for career planning called the Inside Job Model. When you use the Inside Job Model, you go inside yourself and ask, *"What is it I'm interested in, and how do I find opportunities that will inspire me to love my work?"* You begin to look for work that will fit you properly, comfortably, and with joy. And, as we learned in Secret One, happy people are more engaged in their work and more successful financially.

There are four key components to the Inside Job Model that will help you to love your work and thrive in any economy. It's adaptable to all stages of your life, making work-life balance a reality and no longer a question.

Think of the four components of the Inside Job Model as though you are building a house (please see Figure 1). You have your foundation, which is Career Design; the two walls, Experience and Parameters; and the roof, which is your skill base. No career move or transition should take place until you have your house in order. Missing even one of these walls will profoundly affect your ability to adapt to and change your career transitions smoothly and effectively.

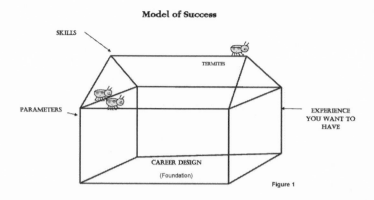

Figure 1

Career Design

The foundation of your house is your unique Career Design. Most likely, you are reading this book right now because you are experiencing a significant life transition. Perhaps you are, or are about to be, between jobs; you have been laid-off or are simply done with the work you do now; you are a college graduate entering the workforce for the first time or you are re-entering the workforce after a hiatus: You are desiring—or being forced into—change. No matter what is happening with the economy, knowing your Career Design will make you resilient: You will be employable anywhere at any time, because you will not only know how to adapt your design to new and different work situations as needed, but you will find that new job opportunities will find you. Career Design is what keeps you grounded and focused on the things that you are passionate about—without it, your career house may be somewhat rickety and shaky. Secret Eight is all about Career Design and will show you how to begin to uncover yours.

The Experience You Want to Have

The next thing to consider is the wall on the right, marked Experience You Want To Have. Most of the time, we don't ask ourselves, "*What is the experience I want to have at work?*" or "*How do I want work to feel?*" "*Do I want intellectual stimulation? A collaborative team? Time alone? Excitement? Calm?*" The answers to these questions will change as we change over time, and they will play a very big part in deciding who we want to work for and where. As long as we negate the experience we want to have at work and are focused on getting the next job, we will continue to make the same choices that are not aligned with our career design. When we are disconnected from our feelings, we lose our ability to correct misguided directions. Once you are clear about the experience you want to have, more choices become available to you and greater success is available. We talk more about how to use experience as your career guide in Secret Seven.

The third wall is about the parameters that will allow you to relax and have peace of mind while you work.

Personal Parameters

The wall on the left is marked Parameters, short for personal parameters. With the Inside Job Model, you ask the questions, "*What kind of life do I want to lead?*" *What do I need in my life to be healthy, happy, and balanced?*" The answer to those questions will also change throughout your life. For instance, Ana's normal waking hour is somewhere between 3:30 a.m. and 4:30 a.m. For her day to be complete, she begins her early mornings by walking her dogs, working out, and spending a few minutes with her husband. She's planned her entire working schedule around her natural sleep patterns and desire to connect with her four-legged animals and beloved husband. At this point in her life, the standard working hours of 8-5 do not work for her. Exercise, sleep, health, and connections are all a part of our daily lives. The experiences we need to maintain health, wellness, and balance of the spirit and body are often negated in the standard career planning model. With the Inside Job Model, personal parameters are essential to career success and abundance. And yes ... you can find work that will meet your personal parameters. You just need to incorporate these parameters into your job search to create this kind of life for yourself.

Transferable Skills

The roof of your career house is comprised of your transferable skills, all the experiences in your life that have value, whether paid or unpaid, professional or volunteer, pleasant or unpleasant. Throughout your life, you have accumulated transferable skills that can be used (or not) in a variety of ways. So often, we negate our skills because we weren't paid or validated for acquiring them or they seem so common that we assume no one will value them. The Inside Job Model values all that you bring to every situation. Every tile on your roof is comprised of a skill that has been acquired since you were a child. By taking a cohesive inventory of all your skills and then choosing the ones you want to use, being clear about what you don't want to use and which skills you may want to enhance with additional training, you acquire a portfolio of talents that can be used in many ways. For instance, Mark can read blueprints, and Carrie was a radio disc jockey for six years, but Mark doesn't want to do work that involves reading blueprints, and Carrie doesn't want to sit in a radio booth and talk to people she can't see. Yet Mark's eye for detail and Carrie's communication skills serve each of them every day in so many capacities. Transferable skills are often your career flotation device that keeps you buoyant on the waves of change that so often come your way.

The Termites Eating Away at Your House

Did you notice the little bugs on the house in Figure 1? Those are the negative thoughts we call termites that eat away at the framework of your inner house of dreams. These termites are based on myths or habituated thoughts (Secret Four) that often show up as *shoulds, have tos* and *yes, buts* as in: "Yes, I'd like to work part time, but I *have* to work 40 hours a week." Or "I'd like to take a year off and travel, but I *should* be going to school." Or "What I really want to do is be an animal trainer, but my parents, who I adore, are going to be so disappointed that I *have* to become an attorney." "I'd like to be a musician, but I'll never make money at it."

Where would our culture be today if Steve Jobs said, "I'd like to build Apple computers, but first I have to finish college," or if Oprah Winfrey had said, "I'd like to become a world-famous talk show host, but it will never happen because I'm a black woman?" Overcoming termites is our greatest challenge to building a strong home inside ourselves. These thoughts will tear down anything you build, if you let them.

When she owned a retail store, Ellie did a powerful experiment in shoulds and have tos. *"I noticed I was not having much fun or satisfaction at work, and I felt overwhelmed by all the 'should' do's in my life. So because I owned the place and it was Lent, I decided to give up doing anything I should or had to for 40 days. I had not been raised religiously and never saw the point of Lent in the past, but the idea popped into my head and, just like that, I was committed. Now I was in a pickle. I had a business to run which involved feeding and caring for animals and a staff of 12 who depended on me. I had to figure out how to accomplish what there was to do without doing it from should or have to.*

"The first week was horrible. It was as though I had no life other than should or have tos. Then I noticed something. My stress level went down, and I became interested in my work again. I began to hear a different guidance system, the one that comes from Divine Wisdom. I got more accomplished in less time and was much easier to be around. My work took off, and I never again let should or have to have power over me."

Every time you think should or have to about work you close potential opportunities for yourself without even considering them. We're not suggesting that you take shoulds and have tos out of your vocabulary. There are realities of life, and "doing the right thing" can supersede what you most need or want in the moment. But when it comes to long-term, conscious planning about your life and career, these termites, when they appear, can act as red flags, a warning that you may be limiting your thinking and your options by letting these little, itty bitty bugs affect the quality of your life.

And Tam? *"To be able to have the gift of insight into my design and the four [walls] of career planning changed my entire perspective on how I view the world. I say this gift of understanding is priceless. Because of the interwoven aspects of the CWI Master Series program, I felt that all the pieces of my professional and personal life now made perfect sense. This is not a [pie]-in-the-sky type of theoretical program. The Master Series is relevant, mindful, and makes career satisfaction and happiness attainable. If individuals are willing to stay the course and do the work, they will discover the best parts of themselves. The path I am currently on just feels right for me. I am now leveraging my years of experience in marketing and branding with my natural gifts of visual alignment to help individuals harness the true power of their personal story (elements of their distinctive brand) to inspire and do good. As a Visual Image Architect, I have launched my own personal branding and image development company that includes personal brand development. I am forever changed."*

This Inside Job model will help you to discover from the inside out how to find a career that will bring you abundance and keep you interested and happy throughout your entire professional life. Your friends, family, aunts, uncles, doctor, mail clerk, and just about everyone will have an opinion about what you *should* be doing and how you *should* be doing it. Just remember to live inside the house you are creating for yourself and only invite those in who can support you in this process.

SECRET #3

Jumping Off the Corporate/Success Ladder

"Normal is nothing more than a cycle on a washing machine."
Whoopi Goldberg

"To everything there is a season and a time to every purpose under heaven."
Ecclesiastes 3:1

Mike was distraught when he walked through the doors of the Career Wisdom Institute because he had just been laid off. He was 45 years old and a respected Vice President of Business Development and Product Marketing for a high-tech firm. His career path looked pretty typical and was filled with success. He started over 20 years ago as a marketing director at a telecom company and has been moving up the corporate ladder ever since. In addition to his job loss, Mike is going through an awful divorce and custody battle. He has just moved into a one bedroom apartment, had his car towed during a job interview the day before, and was, shall we say, in a very blue mood. He decided to participate in the six-week Master Series through CWI, and while introducing himself to the group of participants, he stood up and walked over to the board. He took a marker and drew a line progressing upward, like a series of steps to heaven. He said, "This is where I started over 25 years ago (pointing to the first step). I've been working my way up and up, making progress, increasing my salary, and then BAM, just like that, I got fired, and all that I have worked for is gone. It's as if it never existed. All the talent I acquired becomes irrelevant. It feels as if I've jumped off the corporate ladder and into an abyss."

The Linear Model of Career Planning

What happened to Mike? Why did he think that all his experience, work, and efforts were now worthless? Why was he feeling so badly about himself, blaming himself, and feeling discouraged? Realistically, Mike is an incredibly valuable asset to any company, but if he can't see through his current negative thoughts about himself and value what his lifetime of professional experience offers, he will not be able to plan his next career move.

Mike was suffering from the belief systems formed by the linear model of career planning. From an early age, we are taught life should look like this: you are born, become educated, married, have children, work some more, retire, and then die. If we follow this path, life is *good*. If we fall off the line or get knocked off and deviate from the trajectory of this linear model by getting divorced, choosing to or being unable to have children, becoming widowed, coming out as gay, or a host of other life events, we are told or assume something *bad* or wrong has happened. This delineation between on the line and off the line promotes the kind of thinking that leaves us feeling poorly about ourselves when things don't go as planned.

That planning begins very early in our lives. *"What are you going to be when you grow up?"* is a question we have been asked since we got out of diapers. Our career paths are laid out before we enter elementary school. We are told we'll find a job, take an entry-level position, and plan on being promoted into the next "higher-level" position and then the next, even if we have no desire or personality skill to do the work. Climbing up the corporate ladder is an expected outcome in any career.

This hierarchical approach to career progression has been referred to as *"The Peter Principle,"* a term Dr. Laurence J. Peter and Raymond Hull formulated to describe the process of being promoted until we reach our level of incompetence. In this linear model, we reach our limits of growth and potentiality by continually climbing the corporate staircase, which often leads to boredom, stagnation, and being fired. It almost seems like insanity, working and scrambling to stay on this linear path of apparent successes and failures that ultimately stresses us out and promotes suffering, especially when we consider there are almost no straight lines in nature...really.

The Career Cycle

Most living things are made up of organic compounds that are polar (unsymmetrical) in nature and do not form "straight lines." Recent research shows that it is not our natural inclination to walk the straight and narrow path, but, in fact, to walk in circles. Scientists in the Multisensory Perception and Action Group at the Max Planck Institute for Biological Cybernetics in Tübingen, Germany, have now presented the first evidence that people really walk in circles when they do not have reliable cues to their walking direction. When not being shown where to walk, we naturally veer to the left and sometimes to the right.

It's ironic that while nature has created a multitude of amazing shapes, patterns, paths, and directions, we humans got stuck thinking we had to walk in one particular "straight ahead" direction. The next time you're walking around taking in the scenery, notice that nature is filled with circles, curves, and spirals. The great architects, mathematicians, and scientists have been studying these curvy phenomena for centuries. Horns, teeth, holes, shells, flowers, bugs, and atoms are all filled with circles, roundedness, and turns. Life is too smart to have provided us with a limited linear existence.

When calm and present, we can begin to see how the very essences of our lives are intricately woven into the circles or cycles of life. These cycles are seen in the weather, menstruation, the moon and sun, relationships, health– and yes, of course, the cycles of our careers (please see Figure 2). There is Spring, a time of birth, inception, beginnings; the Summer of full flowering and accomplishment; an Autumn of harvesting, completion, death, and the time of dormancy in Winter (Renewal and Reflection), where we hibernate, rest, and naturally do nothing. Then spring comes again with her beginnings.

Career Cycle

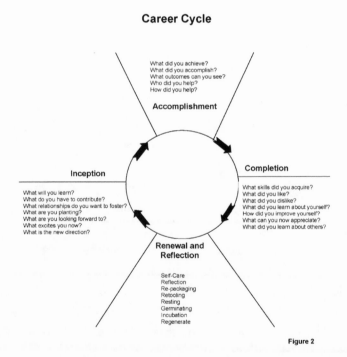

What did you achieve?
What did you accomplish?
What outcomes can you see?
Who did you help?
How did you help?

Accomplishment

Inception

What will you learn?
What do you have to contribute?
What relationships do you want to foster?
What are you planting?
What are you looking forward to?
What excites you now?
What is the new direction?

Completion

What skills did you acquire?
What did you like?
What did you dislike?
What did you learn about yourself?
How did you improve yourself?
What can you now appreciate?
What did you learn about others?

Renewal and Reflection

Self-Care
Reflection
Re-packaging
Retooling
Resting
Germinating
Incubation
Regenerate

Figure 2

Our work in this life is a series of career cycles, spiraling out from our birth until our death (please see Figure 3), always heading in an upward trajectory (reaching for the sun) and overlapping with all the other cycles in our lives, relationships, parenting, health, the cycles of farming, home, and education, which always keeps life interesting.

Understanding this cyclical model of career planning is important because when you see yourself as a work in progress and your career development as a cycle, you start thinking differently about your life. You will know there is no way to make a mistake. Whatever you do will be grist for the next go around. You begin to appreciate all of your experience as capacities and talents you have to offer in

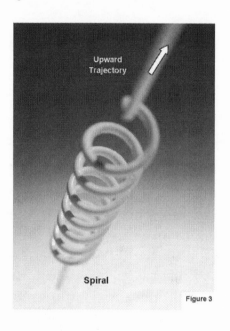

Figure 3

the next job. You see every experience as an addition to the toolbox that you're building all the time. The Career Cycle fosters an appreciation of all situations—even those that are uncomfortable because each season of our cycle offers us something of value.

Once you let go of the linear model's "upward" and "onward" pushing and stress mentality, you will naturally move through the cycle because change is inevitable. Even if you completely check out of life, the cycle is operating. HOW you align with the cycles is up to you. By embracing the cycle and seeing it as a natural part of life, you can take the transitions in your life less personally and rest in the awareness that Spring will come again, even if you don't know exactly when. This knowing can help calm you down and open you up to the wisdom that is available to you at all times.

Completion/The Autumn of the Career Cycle

To begin the discussion of the Career Cycle, we start with the ending. Most people come to the Career Wisdom Institute when something has completed: a job, a marriage, a lifestyle, or perhaps wanting to end their unhappiness. These endings are often filled with complex emotions: sadness, fear, anxiety, and excitement, all which often lead to exhaustion. The truth about endings, however scary they may feel, is that all wisdom and confidence is born by experiencing every part of the cycle. The knowledge you have acquired is valuable to others when you learn to value it in yourself. When you can surrender your fear of losing what appeared to be permanent and stable, you can begin to notice all the skills, knowledge, and information you have acquired and take those into your next venture. This is key in understanding your work as an Inside Job. So many people come to us and say they want a stable job with a company that is secure. They never want their jobs to end. But that kind of job does not exist. All companies experience the same cycles as individuals. If companies are to continue their growth, they cannot remain stagnant. The cycles will occur, and your job will never be permanent. The only job that will ever be secure is the one you have going on inside of you. Your job is to collect experiences, knowledge, and information and then learn how to transfer them to the next opportunity.

There is a basic theory in physics called the Law of Conservation of Energy, which states energy cannot be created or destroyed; it may only be transferred from one form to another.

The total amount of energy never changes. When your job ends, be it through termination, boredom, illness, etc., it simply means it's time for your energy to be transferred into another container, process, or event. This is why taking inventory of your transferable skills and experiences is your first and primary action in times of endings.

Ask yourself:

◊   *What skills did I acquire in this last job?*

◊   *What did I learn about myself?*

◊   *How did I contribute in a unique way?*

◊   *What leadership role did I play?*

◊   *Who did I help? What improvements did I make?*

◊   *What did I like about this experience? What did I dislike?*

◊   *What did I learn about myself?*

◊   *What can I now appreciate that maybe I couldn't have appreciated before?*

◊   *What did I learn about others?*

◊   *What industries could benefit from my skills?*

The answers to these questions will help you to construct the transferable skills "roof" of your Inside Job model mentioned in Secret Two, thereby moving you closer to your next beginning. Often, from a resume perspective, these answers are your summary of qualifications or professional profile. It's more important, though, that you understand how significant and valuable your endings are, even when they hurt.

As endings and completions in our lives are valued and seen as the next healthy thing to do, we are moved into the next phase of the cycle called Rest and Renewal.

Rest and Renewal, when honored and observed, if only for a brief period of time, is where you will discover what to do next.

Rest and Renewal/The Winter of the Career Cycle

We've noticed that an interesting consequence of this really deep economic recession for many of our clients is a relief and almost gratitude for the loss of their job and the involuntary time out. Often, it is in this place between job loss and job discovery that one rediscovers their natural body rhythms (as opposed to the Monday to Friday 8-5 schedule), their health, or their inclinations. No one is telling them when to show up or how far they have to commute. While unemployment can be a time of anxiety, it can also be a time of reconnecting to the self.

This liminal period is the threshold between completion and inception, between endings and beginnings, between one job ending and the next one beginning. Much of what you have come to know, your time schedule, co-workers, commute, even what you eat and when you go to the bathroom is in a state of flux. William Bridges, the author of *Transitions: Making Sense of Life's Changes,* refers to this time out as "the neutral zone." In Buddhism, it's called The Bardo. Farmers think of the time between harvest and planting as allowing the ground to lay fallow, so they rest the soil and prime it to grow again.

In this rushed, overwhelmed, multi-tasking Western culture of ours, we're not used to sitting still or even giving ourselves time outs. However, Mother Nature knows the importance of stopping. If you can give yourself just a small break, even in a time of great and uncomfortable transition, the advantages will far outweigh the initial adjustment.

It is in this in-between place where new ideas come out to play. Just like nature needs the dormancy of winter, we need to create the space to allow different possibilities to emerge and contemplate our options. Then we can be sure that wherever we go next comes from our Design, our deepest desires and longings, not because we can't think of anything else to do or because we've always done it. This phase is the perfect time for conducting informational interviews, networking with old and new contacts, and researching new companies and ideas, as well as business concepts for budding entrepreneurs. It's an opportunity to readjust our body rhythms from the unnatural (for some) Monday through Friday 8-5 routine to one that is more aligned with our lifestyle and pacing. It's time to sleep, reconnect with nature, meditate, contemplate ... per chance to dream.

When embraced, this period of renewal and reflection is also where all new beginnings find their seeds. Any artist will tell you that new ideas are born in this place of great potentiality. Sometimes you just have to stop and breathe to fully recognize and hear all the wisdom that is available to you when you are quiet. If you are looking for a new career path or business idea, this is the place it's going to happen.

Resting Jobs

All that being said and given our financial responsibilities, loans, mortgages, kids in college, and basic life necessities, stopping and resting is not always a possibility. If we cannot take a job time out in our actions, we can do so in how we think about work and what our next steps might be. Consider taking a job that gives you time for the reflection you need. At CWI, we call this a *vacation or resting job*, one that does not require the same energy or intention of a fast-paced, full-time job. Many of our executive-level clients create their resting jobs by becoming contract employees or consultants. As contractors, you are more likely to call the shots in the hours you work, the fees that you charge, and the assignments you take. Your earning power may actually go up, while your stress levels go down! Many consulting careers have started in this space of Rest and Renewal. Others use this time to work in fields that are new and different. One doctor retired and started working as a caterer. A police officer took a stockroom position at a high-end clothing retailer. A life coach began grooming dogs and matched her former salary within six months. A third-grade teacher started tutoring privately and made more money. Resting between jobs can often lead you right into your next professional inception, the Spring of your career cycle.

Inceptions/The Spring of the Career Cycle

The ground has rested, the seeds are planted, and now the beginning emerges. A few months ago, Julie helped two little boys plant sunflower seeds in their garden. The boys called Julie one day to ask, *"Why aren't the flowers growing?"* to which Julie replied, *"Just because you can't see the buds yet, doesn't mean they aren't growing. It's happening, but in the sunflower's own time. So be sure to keep watering your plant, but not too much that they'll drown. Give them room to grow, and provide a safe place to do so. And be sure to mark on the calendar when you planted the seeds so you'll know when to expect their arrival."* She concluded by saying, *"Remember, you don't know if it will grow up straight, curled, bent to one side or another, but you do know it will be a flower and it will be reaching for the sun."*

Each moment and every breath and sunrise offers us an opportunity to begin again. Life is one big do over. The question is not when will things begin, but how will they begin, and that answer is in your hands. On the linear model, filled with goals and checkpoints, we so often expect our beginning to look conclusive, solid, knowable, and tangible. It is from this attempt to make the unknowable knowable that all stress and anticipation arises. It's important to remember that, from the Career Cycle perspective, beginnings are the starting point of a journey. This journey will be guided by your desires, instincts, and willingness to be open. Beginnings are nothing more than the emerging and unfolding of ourselves as we align with what life has in store for us. That kind of alignment comes from allowing ourselves to be moved deeply and inspired to pursue that which interests us.

The path to success is not paved in a straight line that goes from point a to point b. True success comes from focus, effort, grace, synchronous moments, chance meetings, networking, connecting, pushing the boundaries, asking the right questions, trusting your gut, and being passionately interested in the work you are doing. The self-made multi-millionaires of this world do not "fit" into nice little corporate boxes, and many did not have a perfect plan when they started. They are people who have risked for what they love, have jumped before looking, followed their passions, worked hard, studied, laughed, and believed in the capacity of their larger self.

While you were hanging out in the rest and renewal place, you had a chance to develop ideas about what you want to begin. Now in the beginnings, it is time to start asking the questions that will foster your next career move. Before starting your job search, ask yourself the following questions:

◊   *What do I want to learn?*

◊   *What do I have to contribute?*

◊   *What relationships do I want to foster?*

◊   *Who is already doing the work I want to do?*

◊   *Who do I need to meet?*

◊   *What skills do I want to use?*

◊   *What skills do I want to develop?*

◊   *What is the experience I hope to have?*

◊   *What is the new direction in which I am heading?*

◊   *What am I in service of?*

◊   *What do I want to learn?*

◊   *Who do I want to learn from?*

◊   *What skills do I want to develop?*

◊   *Can I volunteer for a period of time?*

◊   *Are there internships available?*

The answers to these questions will help you select jobs you want to pursue, employers you want to work for, and clients you want to attract. As organic as the beginning process is, you still want to take the most active role you can in making your opportunities flourish. An active beginning will always produce more positive results than a passive one. If the land isn't worked and the seeds are not watered, the plant can't grow. Every aspect of life includes this partnership between effort and grace—effort and focus to head in the direction you want, to step through your fears and into courage, to overcome the habits of thoughts that keep you stuck, and to dispel the myths that have encouraged you to suffer. With the "right" effort, the kind that comes from your heart, "grace" has a chance to meet you, and she will do so in ways that are unexpected. When it happens, it will feel like magic— being in the right place at the right time, receiving returned phone calls from employers while you're on vacation, and long-lost contacts showing up out of nowhere. Life steps in to meet you with all her special gifts and surprises.

Beginnings will come more easily if we can remember...

◊   To put one foot in front of the other. Just start walking on the path, following what feels right.

◊   To take in the lessons that life offers. All experience has value, especially the ones we didn't get quite right the first time.

◊ That we don't have all the answers. Allow for "not knowing." We'll learn more this way.

◊ To watch our "wouldas," "couldas," and "shouldas." Ohhh, they keep us stuck in the past and keep us from being present. This doesn't mean losing our code of conduct or ethics, just being sure we're not kicking ourselves for not living on "the line."

◊ To make a commitment to not feel resentful. It was Nelson Mandela that said, "Resentment is like drinking poison and then hoping it will kill your enemies." Doing anything out of resentment will not produce the beginnings you desire.

Accomplishment/The Summer of Career Cycle

Beginnings are often illusive; they are the start of something without knowing the outcome. Accomplishments are your intentions taking form and shape, coming to life and being born into a whole. They are a union of your thoughts, actions, feelings, efforts, and grace, producing a harmonic alignment with wisdom. You are holding in your hand, seeing before your eyes, and feeling in your body what you had hoped would emerge from your beginning.

A "sense of accomplishment" comes when you stop, notice, and give gratitude for what you have achieved and how you have grown as a human being. Take some time to ask yourself the following questions:

◊ *What was the process I used to bring this accomplishment forward?*

◊ *What positive feedback did I receive?*

◊ *What were the tangible measurable results?*

◊ *What benefits did I bring to the table?*

◊   *Did I notice who I helped and who helped me?*

◊   *How did I influence the outcomes?*

◊   *What is new in my life?*

◊   *What is true now that wasn't before?*

◊   *How have I changed?*

◊   *What was I able to let go of?*

◊   *What increased?*

◊   *How have I become more loving?*

◊   *How do I see myself now?*

◊   *How is there more peace in my life?*

◊   *What fears did I walk through?*

◊   *What clarity do I now have?*

Understanding, celebrating, and recognizing all that you have learned and accomplished in this round of the cycle and being able to communicate that to others is key to awareness and the ability to shift and move into other opportunities that will come your way.

Accomplishments are the fuel in the rocket ship, pushing us toward unknown galaxies within ourselves that we are waiting to explore. Along the way, we will meet new people, see sights, and have experiences we could never imagine from our previous vantage point. In our travels up and around the cycle, we leave behind what has been familiar for what will be unknown. We may leave behind belief systems, constructs, habits, co-workers, friends and neighbors, people we have loved dearly, or places that felt like home. It is also likely we will leave behind situations that have never served us well, like abusive relationships, unhealthy habits, and unsupportive environments. And all of this change does not have to happen on a rocket ship, in a new relationship, or even in a new job. When we find the right journey partners— an employer that supports our continued development, a profession that can grow and change as we evolve—then we only need to leave behind our fears and resistance in order to have what we most want.

That shift in awareness, that you are solely responsible for the experiences you are having, is the greatest accomplishment of all. Your Inside Job is always with you, always morphing, growing, and changing as you do. Accomplishments are always available. From the Inside Job perspective, promotions are not handed to you from an external source, a boss, or within the framework of a company. They come from inside of you. Accomplishments are the signal that it is time to move up and into the next phase of your cycle. You are completely in charge of when you get your next "raise" or "advance" to the next level of your growth and development. This is the natural beauty of the career cycle.

As natural and beautiful as the cycle may be, there can be a lot of resistance to moving around and through it. Fear, discomfort, or not knowing your options can keep you spinning in place for an indefinite period of time or jumping around in a frenetic, inconsistent way. How can you tell the difference between spinning and jumping? By how it feels in your body.

Spinning in place

How many times have we stayed in relationships we knew were over? Or how often have we stayed at jobs that we outgrew and no longer found satisfying? We often cling to the stages of our cycles like a person on a ledge of a burning building, our fingertips clinging to the ledge, afraid to let go, and afraid to stay. There are so many reasons we choose to spin in place: Fear, shame, habit, poor self-worth, and our inability to desire more for ourselves. The feelings and reactions associated with spinning range from depression, illness, isolation, overeating, alcoholism, feeling trapped, angry, and confused to simply knowing that you want something different, but don't know how to get it. We think staying with what we know is safer than changing, but, in fact, it is the resistance into the next phase of development that causes financial deprivation and limits our natural capacity to experience unlimited success and abundance. By preventing our own progression, we inhibit the accomplishments that are waiting to emerge from ourselves. Lingering in any stage of the cycle stops us from growing and serving ourselves and others to our fullest capacity.

Jumping around

"Jumpers" are people who won't take the time out to reflect because they feel that they can't, or an opportunity comes along that looks so good they *have* to take it. This jumping like a bunny rabbit from one ending to the next without reflection or even taking a breath before the next beginning can create what we call the "flat tire" effect (please see Figure 4). You thump, thump, thump along, feeling off kilter and never actually calming down. Quite often, poor decisions are made, and the stress and anxiety you were trying to avoid actually becomes worse from making a hasty decision.

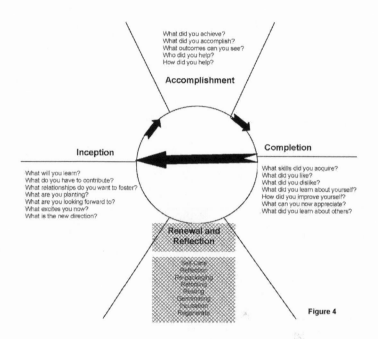

Career Cycle
Flat Tire Effect

Figure 4

So many of our clients at the Career Wisdom Institute are spinning and jumping around and through their career cycle. We see it as our job to gently stop and remind each individual that they are innately healthy and that they can breathe and learn how to transition in a healthy and productive way.

Learning that life is a cycle set something free in Mike. He was able to let go of the self-blame and bitterness over his job loss and realized that a new cycle had begun. He started to work on his thought habits. He took notice of how those thoughts created his experience and began to develop a very deep inventory of his transferable skills. He saw that with every go around in the cycle, whether with work or his relationships, he had increased his knowledge and worth. He developed an appreciation of himself that had been missing for years, and he reconnected with a long-lost love. Mike redesigned his career goals to match the experience he most wanted to have and to use the skills he most wanted to use and develop. He decided to set his focus on working in the green industry, an area he'd been interested in for some time. He used the methods we teach at CWI to create an active job search that led him to a new beginning in his career. His earning power went up in this new industry, and he had more energy to devote as he now loved his work. Mike now knows that work is ultimately an Inside Job and that he can love his work and thrive in any economy.

"Human freedom involves our capacity to pause, to choose the one response toward which we wish to throw our weight."
Rollo May

SECRET #4

Firing the 12-Year-Old
Running Your Work Life

"I won't grow up,
I don't want to wear a tie
And a serious expression
In the middle of July.
And if it means I must prepare
To shoulder burdens with a worried air,
I'll never grow up, never grow up, never grow up
Not me, Not I,
Not me!
So there"
From Peter Pan, Jule Styne

All of us have set points. These are artificial ceilings that limit our ability to be paid well, enjoy our work, be promoted, or be happy at work. These set points are habits of thought that we would never choose if they were on a menu. They go something like this; "The most I can earn is $40, 000 per year." "Women can't do that kind of work." "There's never been anyone without a PhD who held that position." "I'm not CEO material." It goes on and on, and we relate to these set points as if they are true.

True career resilience and freedom comes when we are aware of the thoughts that bind us and keep us from knowing how unique and valuable we are. When we are aware of our habituated thoughts, we are no longer held or controlled by them. Our mature and present self starts running the show.

What's the first thing we do when we cross the street? Look both ways, of course. We do this without thought. It's automatic, a habit, because it's been drilled into our head since we were children. This automatic, habitual, and unconscious process of turning our head is the same way we make career decisions.

When we were born, our brain was a blank slate. As we grew up, the work habits from our family, ancestors, and culture formed belief systems created from a child's perspective that, to this day, influence the decisions we make. Career development begins for most of us after 10-12 years of living in and around these habits. At age 12, the child begins to realize its own individual perspective (let's hear it for teenagers!), yet foundational thoughts about the way the world works have already been deeply imbedded into our consciousness. What we now know from brain research is that repeatedly reinforced belief systems make a physical impact in our brains called neural pathways. These neural pathways are like grooves in our brain (much like grooves on a record). We follow these grooves unconsciously and make decisions on auto pilot about our lives and careers every day from these pathways, without regard to whether or not the decision being made is from habit, thoughtful reflection, or consciousness. In fact, scientists say by the time we're adults, most of our lives are lived in habit. This habituated thinking leads us to make the same immature decisions over and over again as we choose our work or our clients (or life partners) from patterns created in early childhood. What's the definition of insanity? *Doing the same thing over and over again, expecting different results.* Sound familiar?

Neuropsychologist Rick Hanson, author of *Buddha's Brain*, states, *"The brain is like Velcro for negative experiences but Teflon for positive experiences.* For most of us, as we go through the day, most of the moments in life are either neutral or positive. The problem is that neutral or positive moments get remembered with standard memory systems, which is to say they're mostly in-and-out. But negative experiences are instantly registered and intensely focused on, based on the negativity bias of the brain. Then they get stored in what's called 'implicit memory'—not so much memory for events, like what I did on my summer vacation, but rather the feeling of being alive. And that implicit memory bank gets shaded in a darker and darker way by the slowly accumulating residue of negative experiences."

This system was clearly designed to allow us to very rapidly know if a saber-toothed tiger is a pet or a problem, thus allowing us to live so we can experience more of life. However, this unconscious thinking and propensity for the brain to focus on negative experiences are the primary reasons so many of us suffer in our work. It's why we keep being hired by the same cranky boss, choose jobs we end up hating, haven't made the abundant salary we are meant to experience, and feel powerless around our career choices. Our habits are so deeply imbedded into our brains that we truly struggle to make the changes in our lives that will make us happier. As long as we are unconscious about our unconscious thoughts, we will continue to be the victims of our past.

This reality of habituated thinking is why the authors don't believe in career tests which are designed to help people discover a new and different career path. We believe that these tests actually get in the way of discovering what you are uniquely suited to do. If you haven't questioned your habituated thought patterns, you're going to answer the standardized test questions in a way that continues to put you back into the career box you are trying to exit. It's not that we haven't used these tests in the past. Sherry is highly trained in the primary personality and vocational tests. She used to teach and administer career assessments to her clients. They can be interesting and insightful, but are ultimately ineffective in aiding long-term and deep career shifts. The only person who can really answer the question about what you should be doing is you. You really do have all the answers within you.

After working with literally thousands of clients over the last 20 years, we can tell you that most people already know what they want to do with their lives. It's their thoughts and habits that stop them from realizing their own dreams.

Kathy, a 22-year-old, was sent to us by her parents because she was showing signs of depression about her professional future. She was working as a cashier at a hardware store and was not enjoying her work. In fact, she doodled all day long when she had no customers. While taking the Master Series, it was revealed that Kathy's lifelong dream was to be an artist and she had wanted to be one since she was young. Kathy believed the cultural myth that artists can't support themselves or their families, so she never pursued her dream. She became aware of her habits of thought regarding opportunities in the creative professions, and the next thing we knew she had enrolled herself in an online art school. She graduated high in her class, loved the work, and was almost immediately hired by a high-end grocer to do their in-store artwork. She is now training others to do those signs, as well, and she loves her job.

Recent brain research tells us that we can create healthy new habits and watch the old ones atrophy and disappear over time, just by refocusing and being aware.

Dr. Norman Doidge, author of *The Brain That Changes Itself,* explains that our brain "*can change its own structure and function through thought and activity.*" It turns out the brain is plastic and maintains the lifelong ability to reorganize neural pathways based on new experiences. The more positive the experience, the more positive and frequent the outcomes. We go into more detail about this in Secret Five, by the way. The Inside Job plan is that you drop your job titles (the jobs you picked unconsciously) and learn to trust the experiences that feel good to you. It really is that simple. You've walked into an interview before and your gut has told you to run. Or you meet a co-worker and it just "feels right." How about fun? You're doing some activity and it feels good. This means you are in alignment with your Design and having a positive experience. You want to aim to have as many of those as possible.

We are all born with a primal compass, an internal GPS-type system that helps to point us in the direction that will lead to our greatest success and wealth. This innate system is deeply connected to our bodies and sends us guidance through feelings, intuition, and wisdom. Everyone has this built-in system, yet from the moment we are born, we are encouraged to override this fundamental and important rudder through life. *"Tough it out."* *"Work hard."* *"Taking time for yourself is selfish."* *"No one likes a whiney boy."* *"Girls aren't as smart."* We're sure you have a million more habituated thoughts that have been used to shut down your ability to hear your own inner wisdom, thereby shutting down natural opportunities for success.

Through the generations of parents, grandparents, and great grandparents, we have been handed down a *cultural* neural pathway that work is hard, limited, and filled with toil. It's very likely this was true for our ancestors who often came from profound poverty, famine, war, and holocausts. Maybe it's because Adam and Eve got kicked out of the Garden of Eden for taking a day off to enjoy the "fruits" of their labors. Nevertheless, the warning from our descendants has limited our own true success. Try answering the following questions:

◊ What did your mom think about work? How did she describe the work she did to the people she knew?

◊ How did your dad think and feel about work?

◊ If you were lucky enough and can recall your grandparents' attitudes about work, describe those, too.

◊ Do you notice anything? Have you taken on your family's thoughts and feelings about work? Are they yours? Can you make a distinction between how your family felt about work and how you feel about work? When you think about the familial habits about work you've just uncovered, how does your body feel? When you think about how YOU feel about work, do you physically feel different? When you feel a great feeling, stop and consider where it came from. What were you thinking when that feeling showed up?

Again, the thoughts you have around work are most often not based in your present time experience. As you ponder the questions above, you'll begin to see that we have gone about the business of choosing our work with an innocent blindness that comes from our habits of thought. As we said in our preface, awareness of what is running the show will at least allow you to see that there are many more avenues to consider, some which will pay less, some which will pay more, and all of which will be new and could be more satisfying.

If you are working hard at something you dislike or staying at a job that no longer serves you, you will never truly be wildly successful. In fact, the opposite is true. It is positive experience and daily inspiration (joy, fun, challenge, making a difference, loving our work) that gives us limitless opportunity and energy to attain success. If you doubt this, look at the most successful people of our time: The Oprahs, Steve Jobs, Richard Braniffs, and Warren Buffetts of the world. They love what they do and make millions doing it. There is no set *point* on their creativity or the positive experiences they are having.

So, how can we do something about these set points and habits?

Reaction vs. Response

Remember that guidance system that is always trying to get our attention?

When a habituated thought based in childhood fear and assumptions creates a strong reaction in our body, we feel out of control and extreme. Uncontrollable crying, profound anxiety, over-the-top anger or temper tantrums, excessive drinking or overeating, shutting down, and isolating are all examples. Sweating before a job interview, freezing when asked to speak publicly, running away in fear when faced with a big project are all reactive states. The word REACTIVE literally means to reactivate the past. In these moments of strong emotional reactions, we forget that we have the choice of focus and are in complete control over our response to any given situation.

Joe, one of our clients, was stuck in the parking lot, having an anxiety attack because he didn't want to start his first day at a temporary job.

"I've been yanked back into this job, and I don't want to be here." Joe, a high-level executive with a very successful career, was reacting to something from a very old habit, which we were able to uncover using the following three methods:

Breathe: 10 deep breaths is the first thing to do to bring the body back into present time. When we are reactive, we often hold our breath, which sends a signal to the brain that we are dying or gasping for air. The adrenal glands then flood the body in order to prepare it to run, fight, or freeze. The physiology of those states requires that the body send most of the oxygen-rich blood to the core of the body to facilitate all those actions. Guess where the blood is drawn from? Our brains! We literally get more and more oxygen deprived the longer we are in a reactive state. Deep breathing is the quickest way to calm the nervous system. Ten slow and steady breaths (count 4 in and 6 out) re-oxygenates the brain, and we automatically begin to calm back down. Once we are calm, our natural ability to be wise is back at our fingertips. Try this at night when you can't sleep. It's a terrific sleep aid.

Compassionate awareness: When we have reactive thoughts, we often respond to those thoughts with a harsh inner voice. Joe again: *"I'm such a wimp for not wanting to go inside. Why don't I stop being such a baby and just get it over with?"*

These harsh responses only serve to deepen the negative experience, thereby deepening the neural pathways. Compassionate awareness, like breath, calms the mind and the body and allows for self-empathy to enter the picture. You can now begin to hear the harsh critic that lives inside and ask it to be quiet. In this case, when Joe became compassionately aware, he had to laugh at the picture and memory that arose. He could see himself in the first grade, remembering how his mother had to "yank" him into class. His kindergarten class was small, consisting of only 15 kids, while his first-grade class had 65 students. As a little boy who was shy and sensitive, the volume of children in the class felt overwhelming and he felt powerless.

Curiosity: The power of noticing our mood and being interested and curious about our reactive state immediately brings us back into present time, where anxiety and stress cannot live. We are most often worried when we fear the future or lament the past. When we are curious, we are present and begin to deal with what is in front of us. As this client got curious about his reaction, he realized that he was in complete control every step of the way. If he didn't like his temp job, he could leave at anytime. No one was forcing him to go to work. It was his choice, and he became excited about the potential opportunity.

Breathing, Compassion, and Curiosity: it almost seems too easy to believe that gentle kindness toward ourselves can begin to change years of negative thinking. In our culture, where we feel compelled to be doing something all the time, taking action, and controlling events that we perceive as *good* or *bad*, it's important to know that the ability to create real change in our lives ultimately rests in doing nothing more than kindly noticing what has got us spinning in circles. This *being there*, taught by the great spiritual masters of our time, has more impact on changing our brain than we could have ever imagined. Ultimately, it is in the non-doing that all change is truly possible. Our motto at Career Wisdom is "do less, achieve more." As we incorporate these three acts of self-kindness, we naturally begin to bring them into how we treat others and, of course, our work. The awareness to breathe and be compassionate and curious literally brings the word CARE back into career, thus bringing abundance, infinite possibilities, and choice back into our lives.

SECRET #5

Don't Believe Everything You Think

"Throughout time, human beings have experienced insights that spontaneously and completely changed their behavior and their lives, bringing them happiness they previously had thought impossible."
Sydney Banks, 1/25/31 – 5/25/09

"The mind is its own place, and in itself, can make heaven of Hell, and a hell of Heaven."
John Milton

All human beings, every single one of us, are designed with innate health. That health may be covered up by the noise of our lives and our habits of thought, causing us to forget who we are and doubt ourselves, but it's there waiting to be remembered. Our Inside Job is to learn to trust this innate health.

On the physical level, when we bruise or cut ourselves, we know the injury will heal in a few days without us having to "work on it." The same can be said for our psychological health. Our feelings can be hurt one moment and completely fine the next. You can see this clearly with two-year-olds. One moment it's, "I hate *Jimmy, I'm never going to be his friend,*" and 20 minutes later, the children have reconciled and are once again playing together in the sandbox. There was no long therapy session, no blame, just forgiveness and innate health at work.

Remember when you were young and tried to sink your favorite large beach ball in the ocean or the pool? The closer you got to the bottom, the harder it was to hold that ball down; and if you took your eye off it for a minute, it popped to the surface. Well, that's the way we are with our innate health. What's odd is we work really, really, really hard to 'become' healthy and that's backward. What we have to do is let go and let our own innate health rise to the surface so we can think clearly again and get some rest! It is exhausting always pushing so hard on that darned beach ball.

Think of a time when you were angry or frustrated, possibly when quarreling with a work associate. Imagine that your cell phone rang, and it was someone you REALLY wanted to talk to. What happened to your mood? It instantly changed, right? You became this lovely, healthy, engaged and compassionate human being in the blink of an eye. That's how fast the beach ball will rise if you would just let it do so! This access to health and calm is built into everyone.

When we do seminars at the Career Wisdom Institute, we like to hand out snow globes—those fabulous glass balls with winter scenes inside. When you shake them, the winter scene inside the glass is suddenly full of swirling snow. We hand them out to remind people what the inside of their heads look like when they are stressed, but more important, to see how quickly all that static represented by the swirling snow settles when you set the glass ball down and let it rest. Your mind operates in exactly the same way. You get worried and stressed about all the things life can throw at you and bad thoughts start racing like swirling snow in your mind. But wisdom and innate health are under that snow flurry at all times, always giving you guidance if you will settle down and listen to it.

Everyone knows when they are experiencing a good moment or a bad moment because those experiences feel completely different in the body. When you were quarreling in the example above, you were most likely tense, hot, or shaking. When your best friend called, it's likely you felt lighter, cooler, and calm. Awareness of how you feel, recognizing the feeling in the moment, is how you know if you are pushing down on the beach ball, shaking the snow globe, or relaxing and becoming wise. Simply being aware of your feelings will allow innate health to return and stress to be eliminated—not reduced—eliminated.

Yes, you can actually eliminate stress. You don't have to put up with it. You don't have to temper it. You can actually eliminate it by trusting that you were designed to be a resilient, healthy human with peace of mind. It's your birthright to find your way to awareness and keep choosing that healthier experience through three basic principles.

The Principles

There are three fundamental principles that explain how the experience of life works. This understanding calms people down and returns them to their innate health and wisdom. Sydney Banks, who passed away in 2009, was a philosopher and author who discovered the three *principles* that are at the foundation of all human experience.

A principle is something that explains a phenomenon one hundred percent of the time. For instance, gravity is principle-based. There's never a time when you can pick up an object and drop it that it won't fall. Understanding gravity is what allowed the Wright Brothers to be able to build a machine that could overcome gravity enough to fly!

Back to the principles as discovered and taught by Syd Banks:

Principle #1. Divine Thought

If you are alive (and we are assuming you are if you are reading this book), you think.

Our minds were designed to think and to have thought. Syd talked about it as bringing formless energy into the visible world. It seems much like a radio station turned on (to a talk station) all the time. Thoughts seem to come through at a very rapid rate. Several years ago, the National Science Foundation estimated that we think a thousand thoughts per hour. When we write, we think twenty-five hundred thoughts in an hour and a half. The average person thinks about twelve thousand thoughts per day. A deeper thinker, according to this report, puts forth fifty thousand thoughts daily. That's a lot of thinking! All those thoughts are running the show, and we are blind to most of them, even though they have tremendous impact on our lives (see Secret Four). This principle is about the FACT that we think, not WHAT or WHY we think. Ultimately, thought is neutral.

Principle #2. Divine Consciousness

The second principle is the principle of consciousness. Human beings are the only species on our planet that can really step outside of ourselves and watch ourselves think. It's paradoxical, for where do we go to watch ourselves?

We really don't understand how consciousness works, only that we have this ability for self-reflection and observation. UCLA Neuroscientist Daniel Siegal refers to this consciousness as *"mindsight,"* the ability of the mind to be aware of itself and others. Dr. Siegal believes that, *"If you're interested in change, awareness is the place to start. Without awareness, things happen without choice and change occurs without intention."*

Once we become aware of this ability to become self-aware, it makes all the difference in being able to live well or poorly—to be able to watch yourself and make (hopefully compassionate) judgments and course corrections to your life and work.

When we become conscious of our consciousness, we can notice that whatever thought we focus on, we experience. We tend to think that what happens to us circumstantially is what causes us to feel a particular way. But the truth is it's the other way around. It's what you think about what happens to you that determines how you experience any event.

Here's an example:

A client who had gone through our programs and had studied the principles and habits of thought was diagnosed with breast cancer. For 20 minutes, she sat in her car, terrified and upset. She couldn't choose not to have breast cancer, but she remembered she could choose how she experienced the upcoming journey. In that moment, she calmed down and felt at peace. She realized that she could choose her treatment methods and timing, working around her appointments, thus keeping herself interested and engaged in her work, and she could rest when she saw that was necessary. The outcomes were good, and she was able to calm the fears of her family and friends, as well.

Here's how that works. Thought comes through our brain, much like film through a movie projector, and reads out as experience. What we focus on is what we experience 100 percent of the time. If we focus on an anxious thought, we experience anxiety—*100% of the time*. If we focus on a grateful thought, we experience gratitude—*100% of the time*. So if we're having an experience where we're not appreciative or compassionate or we're having an experience where we are cranky, frustrated, or anxious, it's because of the *thought* that we're focusing on, *not the circumstance.* Yes, we really are designed such that the circumstance is NOT what gives us our experience. It is what we focus on that does.

That's interesting. That's an inside-out world. That means you no longer have to try to control the world so tightly. Rather, we recommend you consider just thinking about things in a different way. That awareness alone will allow a flood of new perspectives to come to your mind. But you have to seriously be willing to pretend for a moment that you can't have the habit of thought you normally have.

Caution! We are not suggesting that you "think happy thoughts." In fact, that will only make things much, much worse. We are challenging you to experiment with opening up to new thinking when you have a feeling you don't enjoy. If someone is late and you feel annoyed, think for a moment and see if there is a new way to consider what happened that allows you to feel more even-keeled and balanced—maybe they had an emergency, maybe it wasn't clear when you expected them, or they aren't the right person for that job and that starting time. Maybe the structure could be re-crafted with their help. Keep opening up to another new idea until one comes along that gives you a feeling of interest, rather than frustration. You will then see how to proceed.

This is so important at work. If you look at all our habits of thought around work, most are negative, so it should be no surprise that our experience is going to be negative. This begins to explain the inside out nature of life and work.

Principle #3. Divine Mind

All the intelligence in the world that ever was or ever will be is available to us if we only learn to listen. Some people call this intuition.

Your Inside Job is to learn to hear divine wisdom. When you are cycling through the career cycle (Secret Three), wisdom is most easily accessible during the rest and renewal period. In this place, you can reconnect to the wisdom that is coming from your body, noticing how it is feeling and reflecting on the wise and gentle voice that is always giving you the direction you so often seek from the outside world. When you are researching a company online or interviewing for a job, your body and wisdom is giving you the input you need to make the best decisions for yourself. Poor decisions are made when the input from your body and divine wisdom are overridden by the "should" and "have to" voices/ termites that are often much louder.

Imagine going to a symphony, and when you walk in, all the instruments are already playing. With that wall of noise and music surrounding you, it would be very difficult to hear the piccolo (the little tiny flute) playing in the background. But imagine now that there's a piccolo solo and then the symphony starts to play again. Now you can pick out the piccolo's voice because you've heard it by itself. That is how Divine Wisdom works. Until you come to a reflective and quiet place long enough to hear how Divine Wisdom sounds in your own life, you will continue to miss the key information that will guide your decisions for the Inside Job.

A lovely Chinese Proverb that encompasses the principles is: *"You cannot prevent the birds of sorrow from flying over your head, but you can prevent them from building nests in your hair."* That's true about thought, as well. There's a huge flock of thought flying over your head all the time. Be careful which ones you allow to build nests in your hair.

LeeAnn is an amazing CPA, CFP, wife, mother, and community member. She noticed that she was reticent and anxious when people asked her to take on more and more leadership. After hearing about the principles one weekend, she began to relax and look forward to what might be next. Then she became aware of something amazing.

"Last year, I qualified for the prestigious Blue Chip Council, which pushed me to the top 1% of financial advisors in the nation. Recently, I was asked what I did differently last year that doubled my productivity. It did not take long before I realized that working with the principles is what made the difference."

When I started working with Julie to learn the principles, I knew it would improve my life, but I did not have clear expectations as to how. Soon, magical things started to happen to me as I became more aware of my thoughts and their effect on my experience. I felt less stressed and more in love with life. The way I listened to my family and my clients definitely improved as I became a better listener and communicator. The results were incredible."

Principles Recap

Thought

If you are alive, you are thinking, all the time, like a radio station playing in your head.

Consciousness

You have the ability to tell what experience you are having, just by observing and being aware. You can tell when you are generous, wise, a little dense, or a lot frightened.

What you focus on is what you will experience, 100% of the time. (please see Figure 5.)

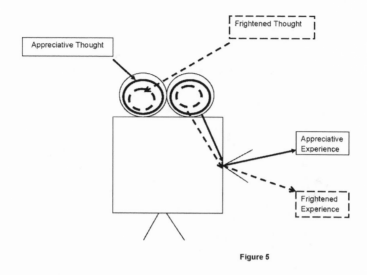

Figure 5

Divine Mind/Wisdom

All the intelligence that ever was or ever will be in the world is available to you if you will learn to calm your mind and be open to Divine Wisdom.

As this principle-based understanding comes alive in each of us, we become the author of our own experience. We find stress dropping away and the ability to again enjoy life and work returning effortlessly. With this newfound hope and interest, discovering satisfying work or great clients becomes something to look forward to and resilience becomes innate. You begin to give up the notion that there is anything wrong with you. You understand that your errors have been innocent errors of misunderstanding and not intent. You recognize innate health and wisdom and how that guides you toward resilience, peace of mind, and an Inside Job.

SECRET #6

Staying in the *Eye* of the Storm

"Peace. It does not mean to be in a place where there is no noise, trouble, or hard work. It means to be in the midst of those things and still be calm in your heart."
Unknown

Our culture is in a very bad mood ... and it's costing us dearly.

"The economy sucks." "There are no jobs." "I'm too old." "No one wants to hire me." "I can't leave this job because I'll never find another one." "I can't make money doing the work I love." "I have to send out at least 20 resumes a week and clearly no one wants me because employers never respond." These are familiar comments we hear day in and day out at the Career Wisdom Institute. What these clients are experiencing are bad moods that are, quite honestly, not true. As the principles teach us (in Secret Five), if those are the thoughts you are thinking, then that will be the reality you experience.

Looking for work or changing careers does not have to be stressful or hard. But *when we navigate a career transition in a low mood, feeling insecure, or pressured by time constraints, then we are working at a diminished capacity.* When we recognize that our mood is a temporary state of mind or feeling, our innate health automatically begins to correct. Just as our bodies heal a cut or tell us when we are having a reactive thought, so, too, can we notice when we are in a hidden habit of *mood*.

Not surprisingly, we tend to energetically absorb our family mood environment. If we grew up around calm, happy moods, then that is our tendency or habit. If we grew up around fear-filled, anxious, angry people, then that is often our unexamined mood. Looking for work requires the awareness to recognize what moods are at play with you, as well as the client or employer.

What mood are you in when you think about changing careers? What mood are you in when you interview? What is your mood when you think about money? Your mood can have a profound effect on the outcome of your job search, interview, and ability to cultivate abundance.

Imagine that you are a hiring manager and your day is filled with six interviews. All of the candidates are qualified based on their resumes and initial phone screenings. The first candidate you meet is so nervous he's sweating; the second is anxious; the third is cranky; the fourth is scared; and the fifth one talks too much. Now it's the last interview of the day, and you are fried. The last candidate sits in the chair and says, "*Wow, looks like you've had a hard day.*" The candidate is in a light and pleasant mood. The next thing you know she says something funny and now your mood has changed. You feel lighter and inspired. Guess what? That relaxed candidate just moved to the top of your list, not because of her skills, but because you like her. When you ask employers why they hire the candidates they do, most will tell you that while skill and experience are important, ultimately, they hire the candidate they like. Likeable people have a can-do energy and inspire confidence in those around them.

According to an article in the December, 2010, MIT Sloan Management Review, researchers Ron Kaniel (Fuqua School of Business, Duke), Cade Massey (Yale School of Management), and

David T. Robinson (Fuqua School) studied the effect of an optimistic disposition on MBA students' job searches and then promotions in the two years after they graduated. The bottom line? *"Optimists fared better than their less-optimistic peers in some important ways, the researchers report in a recent National Bureau of Economic Research working paper. For one thing, the optimistically inclined MBA students found comparable jobs to their peers — but found them more easily, with less-intensive job searches. Even better, two years after graduation, the optimists were more likely than their less-optimistic peers to have been promoted."*

Malcolm Gladwell, author of *The Tipping Point: How Little Things Can Make a Bigger Difference*, was quoted as saying, *"Sociability, energy, and openness breed luck."*

By the way, the resume ´is the tool that gets your foot in the door, and the interview is really only a date. Would you go on a date in a low mood? It's a date between groups of people who are trying to decide if they're going to make a commitment to one another. Who wants to commit to someone who is no fun to be around? That's the power of understanding moods. It can give you a distinct advantage at all stages of your career as you are aware of being in a low mood, then breathe or reflect yourself into a higher one.

Let's look at the powerful Moods for Living (please see Figures 6, 7 and 8). When we begin, it is essential to consider that moods come and go like the weather. It's as though we get into a storm of thought and our moods plummet. There is often no reason for the mood that lands on us. Neurologists have said that if we could see into the brain of someone sitting on a park bench, we would see a constellation of moods pass through that person, even if there was no change externally except the passage of time. Moods just come and go. Recognizing them as only moods will help us wait for them to pass. The secret is to know that if we wait the mood out, another, and probably healthier, one will show up.

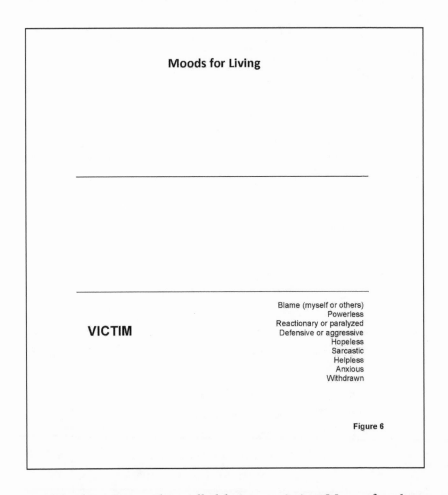

Moods for Living

VICTIM

Blame (myself or others)
Powerless
Reactionary or paralyzed
Defensive or aggressive
Hopeless
Sarcastic
Helpless
Anxious
Withdrawn

Figure 6

The lowest mood is called being a victim. Most of us have spent at least some time wallowing in this territory: *"I'm the victim of the economy," "No one will want to hire me," "No matter how hard I try, it never works out."* There's always a reason that we feel the way we feel, and it's never our fault. When we feel like the victim of anything, we have a tendency to blame. That's the hallmark of that mood; we are either blaming ourselves or blaming others. We feel powerless, reactionary, hopeless, or paralyzed. We feel stuck, helpless, and anxious. Many of our new clients come to us in this mood. We can tell by how they speak. *"I must not be looking hard enough or looking in the right places. I'm too heavy, I'm too stupid..." "I need more education." "The corporations have all the power; the bosses aren't hiring." "I won't even look because if I go out into the world and look for work, I'll just be rejected, anyway."*

No wonder people are so sad and paralyzed. There is a huge victim mentality in times of transition. We don't like change, so we look for something or someone to blame. In fact, most of what the media projects at this point is keeping people victims; they're focusing so much on what's not working that people just keep falling more and more into this habit of being in a victim mood.

The truth is there are a lot of hopeful and amazing things happening right now. Many new companies are being born: eco-companies, environmental companies, solar companies, and car companies. In San Francisco, we're seeing the birth of really creative, conscious businesses, and very few people are talking about that. We recommend that you begin to notice if the source of your information inspires you or depresses you and make a choice toward inspiration.

The victim role is a very powerless and vulnerable mood. When we are uncomfortable, we look for ways to deaden the feeling of pain. Alcohol, comfort food, drugs, or TV may be distractions we reach for because we think this mood is real. We don't realize it is a mood that, if left alone, will pass.

When it finally hits us that the victim thing is not working, people tend to pop out of this mood by being *determined* to get ahead. Next, we most often simply move up to a mood of hyper-responsibility. This is the right direction, so appreciate that! But it can sound like, "I have to work really hard to find a job..I have to..earn a living."

Moods for Living

HYPER-RESPONSIBLE	Hard Work Second Guessing Doing too much Overwhelm 'Press'-energy (Tired, never done) Hopeful Pressure Multi-tasking Action for Action's Sake Reactive
VICTIM	Blame (myself or others) Powerless Reactionary or paralyzed Defensive or aggressive Hopeless Sarcastic Helpless Anxious Withdrawn

Figure 7

This mood still feels physically horrible. This is called the hyper-responsible mood and is where we over-achievers, multi-taskers, and Type-A personalities tend to dwell. If you look now, you might be able to see that this mood is common among corporate executives and parents and is often characterized by the words, "*I have to.*" When you're in this place, it feels like a massive burden resting on your shoulders because, "*Everything is up to me.*" The result is relentless stress, working *really* long hours, always with entirely too much to do, and pressing, pressing, pressing to get it all done.

If the hallmark of the victim mood is blame of self or others, then the hallmark of the hyper-responsible mood is working way too hard and putting everything on our own shoulders. When we are in this mood, we find it perfectly reasonable to work 60 to 80 hour weeks, with no space between our appointments, and having kids who are doing every single thing on the planet, leaving us with no rest and reflection time. We overanalyze, second guess, and spin our wheels. We feel huge amounts of overwhelm and lots of pressure. *"I just have to get it done, have to get it done."* We also have lots of "to do" lists. In fact, we had one client who had lists of his lists. Horrible.

People are exhausted in this mood; they're tired all the time and often can't sleep at night. This is a much more hopeful mood, but it's not the kind of hope you want. This is, *"I hope this works out."* It's not a grace-filled hope; it's more like, *"Oh man, I hope this works out."* It's being on the very edge of life, hurtling around the corners, hoping you don't crash and burn.

The hyper-responsible group believes multi-tasking is a good way to get more done, as though getting more done and efficiency promise us any peace of mind or effectiveness at all. According to new research at Massachusetts Institute of Technology, multi-tasking is problematic because it's impossible for the brain to do. The brain can only do one thing at a time. All those job postings that claim to want multi-taskers are really asking for people who can pretend to take on 20 things at once, when, in fact, their poor brain is doing this stop-start, stop-start, stop-start, thing really, really fast and not accomplishing much of anything.

When we are feeling financial pressure, we often and easily slip into multi-tasking and hard work. The truth is this is a mood, and it only hinders our ability to attain security and a feeling of peace. We do many of the same activities, hoping for a different outcome, and never notice that working harder is pushing us further away from financial security, not bringing us closer to it.

When we become aware and begin to relax a bit, life can take on a new illumination and we can hear new opportunities we might have missed when we were stressed.

Hyper-responsibility is a very hard way to search for a job because you end up with a storm of unfocused activity that never quite gets you anywhere ... except scattered. Overwhelmed types tend to make it to the third interview but never get hired because their attention is focused in so many different places that potential employers don't really get that they're with *them*. And they're also not completely with their job search. Half the time, while they are in that first interview, their mind is still going over all the other applications they have completed. In this mood, we work extra hard, taking action for action's sake because we innocently don't see anything else to do. This is a mood that traps a lot of job seekers. It is exhausting, and there's no way to maintain a steady job search in this mood without burning out. When we tell people they need to make looking for their next career their job right now, they think eight or ten hours a day. No. We mean two hours a day, then take a break. We mean three hours a day and then doing something enjoyable. This do-less, achieve-more perspective is what sustains an effective job search.

When we are in moods of blame or hard work, we are living in an *outside-in* world. It feels like controlling the external circumstances is all up to us. In order to get to an Inside Job, where we let life come to us so we can walk alongside it, instead of fighting it, we cannot be in either the blame or hard work mood. In those lower moods, we strain and press. If we are paying attention, we can feel our poor bodies yelling at us to take a break and relax!

By the way, that determination that has hyper-responsibility seem like such a good idea is actually essential to being successful. Some call it grit or intention. From a graceful mood, that intention is what allows you to soar.

These moods have everything to do with your success in a job search. If you try to find a job in a blaming, angry, powerless mood, then the process will be stressful and you'll feel frustration and find limited opportunities.

The good news is when we quit shaking the snow globe, there is actually a mood that's healthy, normal, and natural for us! We call this mood grace or freedom.

Moods for Living

GRACE/FREEDOM

Interest /curiosity
Flow energy
Guided by Wisdom
Responsive/Open
Resilient
Peace of Mind
Reflection

HYPER-RESPONSIBLE

Hard Work
Second Guessing
Doing too much
Overwhelm
'Press'-energy (Tired, never done)
Hopeful
Pressure
Multi-tasking
Action for Action's Sake
Reactive

VICTIM

Blame (myself or others)
Powerless
Reactionary or paralyzed
Defensive or aggressive
Hopeless
Sarcastic
Helpless
Anxious
Withdrawn

Figure 8

Here we have peace of mind and reflection; we have wisdom and trust; we are open to serendipity and synergy; we have congruence and alignment. It feels great. Rather than multi-tasking, we focus on one thing, get that completed and then start the next. This not only makes us more efficient, but it also feels much less stressful. From the grace mood, we are aligned with something larger than just ourselves. Design is the guiding light when we are in the mood of grace, and we can hear Wisdom as though it is on our i-Pods. We feel more like we are called to something, pulled forward effortlessly and magnetically.

The mood of grace is the only place peace-of-mind can occur. It's the only place reflection can occur, and interestingly enough, it's the only place where people are truly interested and curious. When we are in transition, it's like being in the eye of the storm, rather than in the storm itself. In a hyper-responsible, overwhelmed mood, there is no curiosity. It feels like, *"I don't care why it's happening, just make it stop."* In the victim mood, there is no curiosity at all. But it turns out that curiosity is one of those things that can bump your mood into a more graceful place. If you can truly get curious about something that's happening that you don't like, suddenly your mood shifts automatically into an innately healthy place. Here's an example:

Recovering from losing a job, Bettina was starting a new business. That year, she earned $3,000. Since she lived in the San Francisco Bay Area, a very expensive place to live, she was anxious. Her husband, Ben, was a teacher in California and loved his work. Bettina sat at home worried about finances, and her husband would come home from work, go out in the back yard, swing a golf club and hit weeds—no golf *ball* at all.

While Bettina was angrily counting pennies and making pasta stretch, being the victim of Ben and annoyed about that, her hyper-responsible mood had her try everything she could to spend less and *make* Ben more responsible about money. She harped on him and criticized him. She was rapidly moving back and forth from victim to hyper-responsible *weather* in her head!

One day, Bettina was doing dishes and had this moment of grace where it suddenly occurred to her that she had no idea why Ben was out in the back yard swinging a golf club.

So she went out, sat on the porch, and said, *"Can I ask you a question?"* Of course, Ben looked at her very cautiously. Bettina reassured him and said, *"No, no, no, I really have a serious question this time. I'm not picking on you."* Ben then came and sat down with some amount of trepidation. Bettina asked, *"It looks to me like you're working on something; can you tell me what it is?"*

He spent 45 minutes telling her about his plan to become a golf-pro so they could get out of their financial mess. Bettina started crying and said, *"I had no idea."* Here he was, working so hard at a full-time job and then coming home and perfecting his golf swing so he could make extra money. She had no idea, until she became curious. In that one moment of curiosity, her mood shifted to grace.

One of the things that comes up when we talk about grace is people believe we mean inactivity or that being in grace means being mellow, being laid back, and being happy all the time. Anne called one day a year after working with us to say she had, *"..Lost everything we had ever taught her about being resilient."* This was a young woman who had gone through the loss of a toddler several years prior and had recovered beautifully by becoming aware of the principles and her moods. I asked her what proof she had that she had lost everything we taught her, and she told us that she just couldn't stop crying when she thought about her daughter. I asked her how it felt as she was weeping. She paused a minute and realized that she felt like something was letting go, and there was relief in her sadness. She also said, *"I miss my daughter so much."* As we continued to speak, she began to realize that she was, in fact, in a state of grace, and she suddenly began to laugh through her tears. *"I never knew I could gracefully grieve."*

We grieve the loss of many things, with job loss being one of the most impactful. How we grieve, how we search, is up to our mood. When grace is present, we are completely in present time. There is no stress or pressure if we are present in the moment we are in right now. Worry comes from thinking about the past, and pressure comes from thinking about the future. If we look for peace of mind and resilience as the feeling that lets us know our mood, we will be more successful in noticing the grace mood than if we are looking for happiness.

We're not saying that external circumstances aren't real. We are saying, however, that the circumstances NEVER dictate how you feel about them. NEVER. There are some real "have tos" out there. You have to make sure there isn't broken glass and nails on the floor when you have toddlers. You have to make enough money to feed your family and make sure they have some place to live. It's just that you do not have to allow yourself to be in a hostile mood about those circumstances.

Grace is the mood that allows you to be in present time, and this is the best place from which to interview. This is the best mood to be in to start a job search or look for new clients. Notice that effectiveness is only possible when we are in a graceful mood.

Let's look at a task performed in each of these three different moods. The task is looking for work. A job seeker who is in the mood of a victim says things like, *"Nobody's hiring, I can't find a job anywhere."* If they then move from victim mood to hyper-responsibility, it might look more like, *"Okay, I've sent 20 different resume's out to 20 different employers, and I'm beginning to get some response, but not as much as I want."* If the mood then shifts suddenly to grace, it might be more like, *"This is my design. This is who I am, what I can't help but do. Who can use me? Where will I be best suited?*

Where do I most want to work?" And, *"Where will I be happiest working?"*

It doesn't mean that the job search isn't going to take place—it's just going to take place in a very different mood, and this is the place we want to interview from. If we are in a mood of victim in the interview, we think, *"You'll never like me. You're all jerks. They've got all the power, I have none."* Or our favorite, *"Please sir, may I have a job?"* In the hyper-responsibility mood, the thinking is, *"If I just work hard enough, I might get this job,"* or *"I have to prove myself, prove myself, prove myself."*

In the mood of grace and freedom, it's a combination of wanting to be able to talk about yourself eloquently, but also noticing the mood of the people in the room. You'll be asking good questions, going in prepared and interested. For us, an interview is like a party being thrown in our favor, and we get to be the guest who shows up and has fun and finds out a lot about the company and people. That's a mood of grace.

Who do you think employers like to hire? People in a mood of grace and resilience. When we listen from a mood of grace, we hear things we might have otherwise missed. We hear possibilities, we hear how we can be of service, and we hear when we should not take this job!

Interestingly, you can't *make* yourself move from one mood to another, just like you can't *make* it stop raining. But you can know it is a mood coming from inside of you and get curious about the mood. You can stop and breathe deeply and be compassionately aware of your mood. You can begin to laugh at yourself for having an emotional hurricane in your head, finding yourself yet again in one of the low moods. That curiosity and humor feels entirely different than trying to figure out what's going on that feels so horrible, or using the awareness of your low mood to prove once again that there is something wrong with you. One is entirely intellectual, and the other is being aware of the body's guidance system and how the body feels. Here's where we say, *"Huh, I'm really having a reaction, that's interesting."* If you are truly interested (which is a VERY wise state!), you will notice the feeling in your body is suddenly different and you can begin to think straight again. You get interested in knowing the difference in how it feels to think from your *chin up, only intellectually, and from your chin down, listening to the body's thoughts.* When we are only in our heads and unaware of the feedback from our bodies, we miss the most important messages of all.

That's why learning to recognize the mood we're in is very important. One way to do that is to realize that each one has its own unique way of feeling in our body. We cannot be in a blaming mood and have a pleasant happy feeling inside our body. Nor when we are in hyper-responsible mood will there be a sense of peace and calm. We might feel strong, but there is the additional build up of stress. So when we start to have feelings of exhaustion, a tight chest, shallow breathing, or nervous stomach, those are signs. So is over-eating, insomnia, or sleeping too much. However our own body manages to send us a signal that all is not right in the world, this is a strong indicator that we are not in the place that we actually want to be. Remember, your body will NEVER lie to you! However, your thinking will.

No matter our age or previous work history, coming from grace is about living from the *inside out,* which is a much healthier, resilient, and hopeful way to live, because we get to say what experience we're going to have. When you go to an interview or a networking event, for instance, focused on a thought that says, *"This is going to be really interesting because I get to talk about what I love,"* you're going to have a different experience than if you think, *"I wonder if they're going to like me."* You can even feel the difference in your body when you think, *"This is going to be really interesting."* You stand up straighter and get curious, perhaps even excited, about the encounter. If you are thinking, *"I wonder if I'll fit in?"* you feel self conscious and are dreading it before you even open the door.

Remember, we're talking about being in the state of flow. That's how you *know* you're in grace and in alignment with your Career Design—when you think about it or do it, you have all kinds of energy and feel like you could do it forever. That energy is what makes you so attractive to potential employers.

Living this way takes courage, and it takes persistence. It takes courage frankly because it goes against the great expectation that things *have* to be done. Society really wants us all crammed into that hyper-responsible mood where we all believe that the harder we work, the more successful we will be. That is the norm in this society, and trying to step outside that norm and say *"This is not the experience I want to have"* is not easy. It also takes persistence because society has habits just like we do! But it is possible. Since our experience comes from the *Inside-out*, we each have the option to come from a state of grace with life, rather than blame or even hard work.

SECRET #7

Recalibrating Career Goals

"Forget goals. Value the process."
Jim Bouton

Rick was annoyed. He had created a career that he loved in technology and was very good at it. He worked for a small subsidiary of a large international corporation and enjoyed the company of his team. He did not enjoy the pressure and stress, but with the salary he earned and the prestige of the company, well, stress was to be expected, right? Then the team split apart with new leadership at the international level, and he chose to take a break and look for something new. He got a terrific package and set his goal to relax for a few months, and then find his next job within six months. He went through our programs and began to realize that he is a very goal-oriented guy. So when he wasn't hired within that six-month window, he began to panic. Then he took a job that he KNEW he shouldn't take, even as he was signing the letter. Within another six months he quit, and came back to us to see what had happened.

Here's our biggest secret yet … If you want true success, do not set goals in the usual way! We know this goes against every piece of motivational advice on the planet that tells you to have short-term, long-term, big, and small goals, then work hard to achieve them. But if you want to truly understand what it means to have an Inside Job and thrive, then begin by tossing out your traditional ideas of goal setting.

In physics, "the many worlds" theory states that every event has an infinite number of possible outcomes. Think about that for a minute. For every event in your life, there are infinite ways it could turn out. Why is it we make ourselves crazy by holding on to only one possibility? Our body is comprised of molecules and atoms that are constantly changing and being replaced by the minute. The body you had five years ago is not the same body you have today. Human beings are ever-changing, morphing organisms that have been created by nature to adapt and change to the ever-evolving world. Yet we desperately try to prevent change from happening in so many parts of our lives. We seek the safety of a job and the security of a paycheck, a profession, or employer that will take care of us for the rest of our lives.

The career planning currently taught to our high school and college students is in this goal-setting format. We tell our youth to make great grades, pick the best school, career, and profession and then head full steam ahead, regardless of the *experience* they want. It is organized insanity to plan for a career at age 17 and expect that career to carry you throughout your entire life. It's not that goal-setting itself is wrong. This traditional kind of goal setting does not tie into the natural evolution of change, the power of synchronicity, and the endless opportunities for experiences that shape and affect us deeply, for the better.

In a working paper called *"Goals Gone Wild: The Systematic Side Effects of Over-Prescribing Goals Setting,"* authored by Lisa D. Ordóñez, Eller College of Management, University of Arizona; Maurice E. Schweitzer, Wharton School, University of Pennsylvania; Adam D. Galinsky, Kellogg School of Management, Northwestern University; and Max Bazerman, Harvard Business School, the authors concluded, *"...that the beneficial effects of goal setting have been overstated and that systematic harm caused by goal setting has been largely ignored."* The researchers conclude that *"bad side effects produced by goal-setting programs include a rise in unethical behavior, over-focus on one area while neglecting other parts of the business, distorted risk preferences, corrosion of organizational culture, and reduced intrinsic motivation."* So if you are one of those people who can't answer the question, *"Where do you see yourself in five years?"* take comfort in the fact that it doesn't matter at all to your overall success.

Trust Your Gut

When we talk about *experience*, we are referring once again to the internal compass that resides within our body called feelings. How do you want work to feel? Do you want excitement? Intellectual stimulation? Collaboration? Individual projects? Time alone or with others? Sherry worked with a very successful published author who had been writing for years. When this author was asked, *"What is the experience you most want from work?"* she replied without hesitation, *"To gossip."* After years of writing her books, she was lonely and missed conversation and kibitzing around the water cooler. Now she wanted companionship. She didn't care if she got paid or worked as a volunteer. The experience she wanted most was connection to others.

Sustainable Employment

We sustain our ability to find employment in any economy when we can grow, shift, and change with the events and circumstances happening around us. If we're not careful, the myopic view of the goal keeps our head down and focused on one path, instead of our head up and eyes wide open, noticing what is happening around us. Most of our suffering at work comes from trying to fit into a career path or job box, molding ourselves into someone else's viewpoint of how we should act, be, feel, and communicate. This is why we say that all traditional career counseling is backward. (Find the job title you're going to be, then fit yourself into it.) While this may work in the short run, living inside this job box does not sustain us in the long run.

For one thing, we get bigger and we outgrow the box. Soon, we feel cramped and uncomfortable. We miss the sun shining on our face, we want to meet people who live outside our box, and we want to explore and experience. Living in a box is downright uncomfortable, and in the long run, we cannot have a full life in that box. Eventually, there is a yearning to live and be seen outside of the confines of the goals we have been told to set for ourselves.

The Intuitive Career Path

Focusing on the experience and feeling we desire in our career is a key component to developing a life filled with work that will sustain us both financially and spiritually. It will direct us to the employers we want to work for (and who will be seeking us out), the office environment we desire, the clients we want to attract, and the opportunities that are all around us. Ultimately, though, to live the life of sustainable career abundance, we are going to have to trust the one person who truly knows the way ... *ourselves*. We're going to have to turn off the television that tells us the economy is tanking. We're going to have to stop being influenced by other people's fears. And we're going to have to learn how to put our *"own oxygen mask on first."* This is not about becoming selfish; it's about becoming self-focused. You already have all the answers to all of the questions you ask. You just need to trust what you hear and already know to be true, then learn to start following that guidance. If you're going to pick a goal, that's the one to follow.

In the examples below, we share the process we created at the Career Wisdom Institute that has helped hundreds of clients develop the kind of clarity they seek when looking for new career paths and sustainable employment.

We created this process in our very first "Secrets to Career Success" seminar back in 2009. A gentlemen in attendance explained that he had a goal to take his son skiing 22 times that season and had failed because he'd only taken his son skiing 18 times.

We asked him, *"Well, what was the experience you wanted to have in taking your son skiing 22 times?"* and he said, *"I wanted to become closer to him. I wanted us to have more time together. I wanted him to become a better skier, and I wanted me to become a better skier."*

Then we asked him, *"Did you become a better skier?"* and he said, *"Yes."* *"Did your son become a better skier?"* He said, *"Yes."* *"Did you become closer and spend more time with each other?"* and he said, *"Yes."*

"So were you ultimately successful in having the experience you wanted to have?" and he said with bright and cheerful eyes, *"Yes!"* In that moment, he realized how successful he was and was able to let go of this thought that he had somehow failed himself and his son.

Private Sector Bad. Nonprofit Sector Good.

We were working with Sara, a woman who had been a CFO in a financial investment company for over 15 years. She came to our workshop because she wanted a new career path and felt that the non-profit world would be a better fit. People are always coming to us, saying they want to find a really great job in the non-profit sector because they are seeking a different experience then the one they had in the private sector (see labels on top of labels in their thinking!) For profit—Bad! Not for profit—Good—neither of which are true, of course, for many nonprofits are just as dysfunctional and sometimes more so than the corporate world, and many corporations are incredible places to work, providing a positive and healthy environment. It's the preconceived notions of *good* and *bad* that end up limiting our options. If you don't know what you are truly looking for, then you can end up working someplace that fits your goal but makes you miserable.

This is the process we used with Sara:

Sara's Goal: High-level position in the nonprofit sector

We then asked Sara, "*What is the experience and appeal of working in the nonprofit?*" (Or how would it feel if that goal came true?)To which, she replied:

1. *"The drive for mission, rather than for money;"*
2. *"The feeling I'm doing something good;"*
3. *"A feeling of teamwork;"*
4. *"Passion about the work I'm doing;" and*
5. *"Having a direct connection to the people I'm helping."*

Next, we asked Sara how many of these experiences she currently had in her work and to rate the amount on a scale from 1 to 5, with 1 being, "I don't have any of it currently in my work," to 5 being, "I have the right amount of what I want in my work in this moment." Her rankings are the numbers shown to the right of the list.

1.	*"The drive for mission rather than for money;"*	0
2.	*"The feeling I'm doing something good;"*	0
3.	*"A feeling of teamwork;"*	4
4.	*"Passion about the work I'm doing;"*	4
5.	*"Having a direct connection to the people I'm helping."*	2

From this ranking, Sara realized that she had a good team (4) and people she enjoyed working with in her current job (4). She also really enjoyed her position in the company and her ability to affect change. The biggest "ah ha" for Sara was that she no longer shared the mission of her company (0) or felt like she was doing something good (0).

When she started with the company over 15 years before, there was more interest in helping smaller businesses and there was a deep connection to the community. To promote growth, however, the company changed its focus to large investors, regardless of their social or environmental impact. Sara realized that she no longer shared the company's mission statement and she missed her lack of connection to her local community. With this insight, Sara's new goal was to find a company that shared her values and concern for community and social sustainability. Given the number of companies that also share that mission, Sara realized the limits she set for herself by focusing on the goal of working only in the nonprofit sector. Her job search and potential opportunities for employment had expanded beyond her previous limitations.

Focus on the Experience You Want

When you get clear on the experience you want from work, life, and love and you commit to giving yourself this experience, the cycle of suffering ends. There is an internalized agreement that is made between the heart and the head. Each informs the other, and decisions are made in partnership. Even in the midst of all this economic turmoil, shift, and change, clients are telling us that they are happier than they've been in a long time and are finally having the experience they want, despite their concerns and challenges in finding employment. They're slowing down, enjoying their coffee in the morning, and taking walks. They love the experience of being able to plan their day in a way that is aligned with their body. And YES, this is okay. When the International Labor Organization came along in 1919 and created assembly lines and 40-60 hour work weeks, we stepped in line and left behind the knowledge that the experience we want to have in life is the most important thing. The purpose of living your Inside Job is that you trust this experience. It will lead you to your job, client, and next synchronistic opportunity every time.

We recommend that you do this Experience Exercise to help you recalibrate your goals in all aspects of your life and work. Know the experience you want, and then trust your awareness so that when you see that you're off course, you will automatically correct. You actually do not have to "know" the next step, the next place, because in its endless and fascinating complexity, life will always surprise you. You just have to trust your own wisdom to lead you in life's wonderful and mysterious journey. We use the following exercise at the Career Wisdom Institute and in the previous examples. Try it for yourself and discover what it is you are truly seeking to give yourself. Goal-setting is VERY powerful when this Experience Exercise is used first to clarify your true desires and then action is taken to make it all happen.

> *"Success isn't a result of spontaneous combustion.*
> *You must set yourself on fire."*
> Arnold H. Glasgow

Goals or Experience

Please write down a goal you've set for yourself and hope to achieve.

Now please list what you hope to experience when you achieve this goal. Be as precise and explicit as you can be. Generic words like "free" and "happy" need to be defined as specifically as you can. How would that feel in your body if you were free or happy?

1.

2.

3.

4.

5.

6.

7.

8.

9.

10.

Now, go back and on the right-hand side, rate how much of this experience you currently have in your life on a scale of 1-5, (1 being none or "I don't have any of this currently in my life," and 5 being "I am full and complete with this experience").

The lowest-ranked experiences (1-3) are the actual experiences you are looking to have more of in your life.

For instance, if you listed a goal that you want to work for a gaming company within the next three months, you would then list what it would feel like to do that.

How it would feel if that occurred	How much I currently have in my life (1-5)
1. Creativity	4
2. Innovation	3
3. Autonomy	1
4. Freedom	2
5. Purpose	1
6. Flexibility	1
7. Security	3
8. Collaboration	4
9. Belonging	4
10. Education	4

In this case, the items you have less of (Autonomy, Freedom, Purpose and Flexibility) are what you actually are longing to have more of in life and in work. Inside Job starts with the experience you most want as essential parameters to your next career.

Be careful of the termite that follows this exercise! It usually goes something like: *"But there's no such thing as a job that can provide me with the experiences I most want to have in life."* We hear this all the time. It is the very thing that keeps the new beginning from, well, beginning! Now you know the biggest Secret yet about truly effective goal setting. Remember...

> the truth is, setting a goal makes no promise that you will be happy if you achieve that goal,

> the truth is, setting a goal can unconsciously give you more of you don't want,

> the truth is, what we say we want is actually not what we want at all, most of the time.

SECRET #8

The Value of Being Yourself

"I will work in my own way, according to the light that is in me."
Lydia Maria Child, 1843

*"We're all called. If you are here breathing, you have a contribution
to make. There is no greater gift that you can give or receive
than to honor your calling. It's why you were born.
And how you become most truly alive."*
Oprah Winfrey

Career Design is an innate gift you're born with. It's like having brown hair and blue eyes; it's not something that you invented, so you can't really mess it up. Every single one of us has our own Design, and every single Design that was ever brought into the world has its own intrinsic value. Our job as individuals is to understand what our Design is and discover how we can apply who we are through work in ways that both give us great joy and deliver our own unique contribution to the world at large. So actually the crucial career question for each of us is not, *"Where are the good jobs,"* but *"How am I unique, and where can I put that uniqueness to work?"*

We found a story that illustrates this in a very moving way. It's the story of a golden retriever and her service dog trainer, Judy. Judy has a Puppy Prodigy program in which she trains a puppy from the time it's about two weeks old until it's four to six months old and ready to go into a formal training program. The purpose of this training is to have each dog serve disabled people, and to help each individual puppy find its best way of being trained and formed. The dogs learn to open refrigerators, turn on lights, pick up dropped objects, steady people as they walk, etc.

Ricochet, a baby golden retriever, was a true puppy prodigy. She was easy to train and bright and loved her work, but as she got to be six to eight months old, she chased birds. That would be detrimental to the safety of a disabled person who depends on her, so they had to wash her out of the program. Judy was devastated as Ricochet was one of the best students she had ever had. But then Judy noticed something about Ricochet, which is she loved to *surf*.

So they started all over, teaching Ricochet to surf and following her design as they worked with her to become a surf dog. She has now become a world-wide phenomenon as one of the only surfing dogs in the world who uses her ability to fundraise for charity. When she surfs with her disabled clients, Ricochet is so focused she doesn't even notice the birds around her. She immediately supports the paralyzed surfers who slip off the board, and she counter-balances their weight to help them surf successfully. She takes her job very seriously. Judy, her trainer, was smart enough to understand the design of this dog, and Ricochet has now earned over $150,000 in charitable funds for people who are paralyzed. She surfs with the paralyzed people and earns money for their recovery.

This story could have had a different ending, placing Ricochet as a pet and never having her thrive at what she was designed to do, which was surf and take care of disabled people. It shows the left turn that life can take and how open we must be to what life wants from us and our design. Often, this turn is gradual, with one foot in front of the other until we look back at life and notice it is completely different from the image we had in our head when we were young. And we love it! If you want to see the video, please go to www.SurfDogRicochet.com and click on the video that went viral on YouTube™.

As Ricochet's story shows, moments of job and life upheaval are an invitation to become buoyant. Regardless of what is happening with the economy, knowing your Career Design will make you resilient: When jobs disappear, Design is still there. Your Design is not your job title or your outlet for creative expression. Understanding this will make you employable anywhere at any time, because you will not only know how to adapt your design to new and different work situations, but you will find that new job opportunities will find you. All graduates of the CWI Master Series learn how to introduce themselves from Design and not from skills or titles. Who you are is *always* more interesting and provocative than what you call yourself.

What Planet Are You From?

When you truly understand your Design, you essentially describe the planet you live on—how you like things to be, what matters to you and what doesn't, what makes up the atmosphere and terrain. Knowing this not only helps you figure out what you're here to do, but also helps you recognize that not everyone is like you.

The Career Design for Anna, one of our clients, is *bringing spirituality and reflective space to chaos.* She is the Queen Bee of the Organizational Planet, highly organized from her schedule to her tea cups, her planet works for her. However, if Anna thinks that her husband ought to also live on the Organizational Planet, she is going to be one unhappy woman and she's going to make his life miserable, because he lives on *his* planet. Understanding that each of us is designed for different passions, concerns, and talents makes relationships easier, both at work and at home.

Knowing your Design is empowering, not just in terms of your career, but in all of your life because when you understand the concept of Design, you see there really is no separation between the work you do and the life you lead. Many of us struggle with trying to properly "balance" life and work, as if those are two separate issues. At CWI, we believe that when others are talking about work-life balance, they often end up with work-life compromise. They are willing to settle for, *"It's okay for me to hate my job if the rest of my life is okay."* But that approach doesn't truly bring us happiness. Peace of mind comes from finding the congruency and enjoyment in all things, in both work and personal life, and that congruency comes from making your Design the solid foundation for everything you do.

This means that you must throw out generic ideas about good and bad jobs and focus on discovering the kind of job that would really fit with your personal Design. One way to think about what you're looking for is what's called flow.

Flow is a mental state that was first identified by psychologist Mihaly Csikszentmihalyi ("Call me Mike," he says to everyone he meets). Mike discovered what he called flow, which is a joyful state in which you are fully immersed in doing something, and there is a feeling of energized focus, full involvement, and success in the process of the activity. In fact, you are so engrossed in what you are doing that you lose all sense of time or self-consciousness. This activity is neither too hard nor too easy, and it feels so good to do that it is intrinsically rewarding—meaning you want to do it for its own sake.

The activities that create flow are different for each individual, but one of Mike's most important findings is that people are more likely to experience flow at work than at play. In *Beyond Boredom and Anxiety*, he wrote, *"There is no reason to believe any longer that only irrelevant 'play' can be enjoyed, while the serious business of life must be borne as a burdensome cross. Once we realize that the boundaries between work and play are artificial, we can take matters in hand and begin the...task of making life more livable."*

When you experience this flow, we believe it is a powerful clue that what you are doing is part of your Unique Design. It feels so good because it is in your unique nature to do it!

Here's what Design sounds like. Noah, whose Design is being a specialist in "What if?", as well as making the intangible tangible, once told us, *"When I'm up there teaching, interacting with students, helping them to make sense of the information in the way that works for them, I couldn't care less about time. I can have office hours for five hours afterwards and sit there and talk, and I don't even need to eat. It's like this work is my food!"*

> *"Your work is to discover your work*
> *and then with all your heart give yourself to it."*
> The Buddha

When you recognize that we are each born whole, you will understand that you were meant to be just who you are. No one else in the world resonates at your energy level. No one else sees what you see (really). You are one of a kind. Once you come to grasp your Career Design, you'll begin to see how it's the foundation you've always lived from, since the moment you were born.

You Can't Help but Do It Because It's Who You Are

Have you ever felt like the stork had a very twisted sense of humor and dropped you off in the wrong house? If so, you're in good company as so many of our clients grew up feeling like they didn't quite "fit" in with their other family members. That's why we so often grow up feeling misunderstood or out of place, and we take those feelings right into the workplace, too. Yet, it is the very awareness of your differences from those around you that can provide insight into who you really are. The contrast throws your uniqueness into the light of your awareness.

So why can't we hear this design if it so unique to us? As we've shown in this book of Secrets, our brain is filled with habituated thoughts and moods which have their own neurological pathways, ideas that solidify around the age of twelve. These old ideas obscure our view of our perfect Design. As we peel away our myths and thinking about ourselves, Design begins to shine to the surface, and often it is met with some pretty interesting reactions. During the Master Series when people begin to get their Design, there is often a celebratory feeling on one hand, while others greet their Design with disdain and skepticism. "What the hell am I supposed to do with this? How do I make money doing this?" and it's said with a lot of frustration and a lack of self-respect. Upon reflection, people then slowly begin to say, *"Huh, it's true, I actually have been doing this all my life, I just didn't think it had value."* Or, *"Because it wasn't hard, I didn't think I could use it or there was anything special about it,"* and actually that's the piece that we're looking for. We're looking for this Design, this very unique gift, so we can help people figure out how to find ease and grace in the workplace.

It has been said that we parent ourselves as we were parented, and how you greet your special gifts in present time is probably how those gifts were greeted in your family of origin. There is no blame. It's not good or bad; it's just interesting to notice that the way we receive ourselves is often how we are received by others. While going through this process of self-discovery, we recommend that you begin to listen for Design by staying open and curious, which will keep you in a more resilient mood.

The principle of our intrinsic unique nature was beautifully described by James Hillman in his book, *The Soul's Code*, in what he called the Acorn Theory. This theory states that all people already hold the potential for the unique possibilities inside themselves, much as an acorn holds the pattern for an oak tree. He believed that the individual energy of the soul is contained within each human being, displayed throughout their life and shown in their calling and life's work when it is fully actualized.

If you ask parents of young children, they will often tell you that before their kids were born, they thought their children would pop out as tiny blank slates waiting to be molded by them into individuals. That illusion disappears very quickly, however, when they discover that their children come into this world with their own, distinct personalities. Very quickly you can see the seeds of their kind of tree contained within, just waiting for the opportunity to emerge.

The good news is that, like an acorn, who we are is still in there and has been operating all this time. Perhaps this is why so many young people are drawn to this wisdom in a Marvel™ comic book series called X-Men™ that is very popular with young kids (and a few of us adults). The heroes of the comic all have their own mutant power and are seen by society as weird and threatening. Kids love these comics because they go right to heart of our real identity issues—what is your mutant power? How do you show up in your own unique way? That's what we're looking for, your mutant power, your one-of-a-kind Career Design. When you see it this way, the question is not about good jobs or bad jobs, but rather "What is my unique work, and what are all the different ways design can be expressed?"

Lorenzo is a 27-year-old fashion design student. He is a leading shop manager for Michael Kors at Bloomingdales in Aventura, Florida and has been promoted three times since making his career shift. It's hard to believe that two years ago he was a Miami Beach Police Officer walking a beat and arresting bad guys.

How did Lorenzo get from the squad car to the runway? He went from the traditional outside in career plan to the Inside Job life. This shift was not easy for a young Latin man whose parents both worked for the city for over 20 years and clearly rejected Lorenzo for being gay.

Growing up, Lorenzo's love of movement, exploration, design, and diversity was hidden from his family. Negative cultural stereotypes, school bullying, and *"don't ask don't tell policies"* at the police academy only added to the layers of self-doubt and barriers that prevented Lorenzo from loving his work and thriving.

It was Lorenzo's new partner who brought him to the Career Wisdom Institute (CWI) out of concern that Lorenzo's misalignment as a police officer might get him killed. We immediately started bringing awareness to Lorenzo's habits of thought, taught him the principles and the Moods Platform, and helped him to trust the natural guidance system of his body.

We also uncovered the *why* of work, asking Lorenzo to consider what he was in service of in all aspects of his life. Not surprising, he was in service of freedom of expression, that everyone recognize and express their beauty inside and out. It became clear in our six weeks together that Lorenzo's design was a "creative revolutionary" using art, movement, beauty, color, and light to create change and move people toward each other in community and deeply as individuals. For Lorenzo, that meant following his true heart's passion ... clothing design.

As his design emerged with greater clarity, Lorenzo quit the police force and returned to school for a second bachelor's degree in fashion and design. We then focused his new resume toward a job in the retail industry, using his police officer's work history and transferable skills. This was easier than you may think. We are always living our design, even if it's not in the ideal ways. Retail requires excellent customer relations skills, an "eye" for what the client wants and needs, plus thinking and moving on your feet, all of which Lorenzo did in abundance as a police officer. He was trustworthy, pleasant, polite, funny, and not easily intimidated, which are all good transferable skills for any industry.

Lorenzo's first job in retail was as a stock clerk for Michael Kors, and in just a year, he has been promoted many times and is considering interviewing for another position in the New York City branch. He just designed his first dress and had his first runway show. He is ecstatic.

Lorenzo is still peeling away the years of self-doubt and habituated thinking that comes with all of that, but he now knows that he is innately healthy and is learning to trust his inner wisdom. The most important thing Lorenzo has learned in this journey is that work is always an Inside Job, and regardless of the situation, life is filled with abundance and opportunity.[1]

Who Were You Born to Be?

We're not here to tell you what to do for work or how to do it, because the only thing that is truly meaningful is for you to begin to identify the voice you have inside of you that is desperately trying to guide you on your path. It's always there guiding you. You just need to learn how to hear it. When you do, you'll recognize it as yours because it's not like all those doubting, worrying, judging thoughts running through your mind (which,

---

[1] *** It's important to note that employers in this country have the legal right to fire employees for being homosexual or transgender. 29 states can legally fire someone solely because they're lesbian, gay, or bisexual; in 34 states, it is legal to fire someone solely for being transgender. ***

not surprisingly, often sound like your mother or father's voice). Rather, wisdom will sound loving, gentle, and kind because it's always on your side.

We invite you to answer the following eight questions. Taken together, they should give you a lot of information toward discovering your Career Design. We suggest you take the time to write down your answers so you can look at them and see the pattern. Don't rush this, and wait until you have complete quiet and are in a wonderful mood.

Please answer these questions from a *wholly positive outlook.* So no answers to number two like, *"I'm always thinking I'm not good enough"* or any other negative, self-defeating thoughts. Remember, your Design points to what's right about you, even if you've felt up till now that it's wrong. So we're challenging you to look at yourself from that positive perspective here.

1. If you were dropped from an airplane into a foreign country that you have never been to before and did not speak the language, what would you do first?

   Example: you might notice the lay of the land first, where the lakes and roads are, the overview.

2. What's the thing that you do that you can't help but do?

   Example: I see patterns in everything.

3. What fascinates you more than anything else on earth?

   Example: Systems fascinate me.

4. What do you always notice first?

Example: I notice people who have light, buoyant energy around them and teams who are collaborating.

5. When you walk into a bookstore, what section do you go to first? And if you say, "Self-Help," which a lot of people do, then what part of Self-Help? Another way to think of this question is: if I were to go to your house and just look at the titles of the books on your bookshelf, what would I see?

   Example: Mysticism, Human Development, Judaism.

6. What do you think about more than anything else?

   Example: I think, What's possible in this circumstance? And I look for Inspiration.

7. In an emergency, how do you respond? Remember—a positive answer. We don't want you to say, "I freeze." That's not helpful. We want you to answer, what's the thing that you bring to an emergency?

   Example: Step back, analyze the system and overview, calm things down, take charge.

8. What made you unique in your family—not what was wrong with you, but what made you unique?

   Example: I made decisions and led in the absence of leadership. I collaborated through inspiring people.

Here's an example of how one of our clients answered the questions. Noah said that if he was *dropped from an airplane, the first thing he would do* is listen to people's conversations and try to pick up a few expressions in order to blend in. But he would never ask anyone directly how to say something. *"I'd prefer to listen and infer and try to make it seem like I was a part of that fabric."*

What fascinated him more than anything else on earth was, *"Definitely foreign languages, throwing myself into unfamiliar situations, trying to see things from other people's perspectives, imitating people – in the sense of impressions or focusing on people's gestures, how they moved their mouth when speaking, you know, mouth mechanics."*

What do I always notice first?

"The way people speak, their intonation, body language, phrasing, word choices, and grammar. I don't really listen to content as much as notice form, like with the body language that accompanies the words. I'm focused on the way the information is presented and always noticing the verb, subject, all those kinds of things. I can't help but do that all the time."

Needless to say, Noah's fascination with language is an important part of his Design. It turns out Noah *is* a linguistics professor, as well as an accomplished musician, and he can now see that his Design is being expressed in several different and satisfying ways.

Here are five bonus questions to help you gain some more perspective:

1. What do children like about you?
2. What do your best friends say about you?
3. When you help someone, how do you do it? What is your gift to the situation?
4. What really upsets you?
5. What energizes you?

The trick is to answer these questions when you are quiet and reflective. Do them all at once, in a calm and pleasant location. Begin to "hear" yourself taking shape. Do not judge what begins to show up. Write words that touch you, that move you, that strike you internally, and keep that list around so you can consider it as you live and work. Look up those words in a thesaurus and see if there are any words that are similar and are even more accurate to describe who you are beginning to know yourself to be. The thing that will stop this process in its tracks is measuring your answers against how useful they are. Don't do that, please—it will only delay your design from showing up. Get curious and excited about this thing that you can't help doing. Share it with dear friends. Try talking about it with your family. Don't listen to negative comments. Ask ahead of time for people to make positive comments only.

There's a game we used to play as children where we had two pictures side by side that seemed the same. The challenge was to find a certain number of differences. If you could find them all, you won the game! Finding your unique design uses similar skills and insight. There is something so YOU that you don't think it is special. If you look at other people, however, you may begin to notice that what comes easily to you is not easy for your best friend or colleague. You've just noticed something about yourself! Quick, write it down. Invest in a small notebook you can stash in a pocket and as you go about your day, notice what calms you down (write it down), and what interests you. Notice what you are attracted to and what catches your attention, even for a minute. Soon, you'll have not only the answers to the questions above, but also a list of things you've written down to add to the pot.

Spread all of those words and answers out so you can see them. Here's where the skills of another child's game will be helpful. What is the theme of all of those things? What's the same? (please see Figure 9.)

Figure 9

The bat, glove, and baseball are all in the same category. The football is a new category.

We often suggest using colored pens or pencils to circle the things that are the same. Anything that shows an interest in relationship and connection could be red, interest in mystery could be purple, quiet spaces could be green, and interest in how things work could be blue. All of those separate words and answers are not separate things. They are thematic, and the more you can see early themes emerging, the more satisfying this will begin to feel. If you can come up with one overall thing to begin with, that's enough. One person, Kari, started with fascination as the entrance into her design. Through time, there is a refining process that naturally occurs. Now she understands that she can't help being fascinated, and she can't help making truth available to her clients. It turns out she is fascinated because she wants to see a unique truth for each client and circumstance. And it all started with an understanding and reflection on fascination.

As you hang out with your list of words, sentences will begin to form, and your understanding will deepen. Suddenly, you'll be able to notice what excites you and what touches you. It will be as though a layer of gauze has been removed and the real you is finally standing there experiencing life. It may even start to seem silly to judge the gift you were born with, because you didn't choose it—you came with this gift. That's why feeling guilty or selfish or judgmental about who you are and what your Design is makes about as much sense as judging your right arm harshly. You didn't have anything to do with that, either.

When you start to recognize you were designed a particular way—it's not an accident, it's not a mistake—then what? That's an interesting question. You get over being shy, embarrassed, nervous, and anxious about it and declare, *"Well, this is me. I'm going to head that direction and see what happens."* Your job search begins to take on a different flavor, and you notice things both pro and con you might not have noticed in the past. You select things that enhance your ability to do this thing you can't help but do, and you steer clear of opportunities that will thwart that thing.

Working from Design feels good. If you feel consistently angry, bored, or anxious, it could be a clue that you are following someone else's path, not your own, and need to reassess. This can be extremely challenging. One of our clients had just been offered one million dollars a year to run a big division of a corporation. He was sitting there, with pen in hand to sign the contract, but couldn't get himself to do it. He told us, *"My mind kept saying, 'Are you crazy?' Sign the damn thing. But my gut was on fire and every fiber of my being was screaming 'no!' What's wrong with me?"* We helped him realize that his inner wisdom was trying to get his attention through his body, and that even though everyone around him said it was the greatest job in the world, it wasn't the greatest job for him.

We've been on a journey together in this book, carefully having you clear away myths and thoughts that keep you from loving your work and thriving. We've shown you how life is NOT a linear journey, but, in fact, is a series of cycles, all operating from inception, accomplishment, completion, and renewal. Being unaware of what part of the cycle we are about to enter, or have just completed, or trying to skip one sets us up for stress and unhealthy moods. Now that you've begun to understand the experience you want to have at work and can see the importance of identifying the parameters that will allow you to be deeply satisfied while working, you can create new ideas about where your design and skills might be readily used. As reactions arise and you take a moment to breathe and get curious, you will remember that how you experience life is up to you. Your body will settle down while your mood lifts. That's when flow becomes evident and available again and you regain your ability to thrive.

Now it's time to create your Model of Success! (Secret Two) Please fill in the following:

My name is _____

and my Career Design is (Secret 8) _____

_____

_____

_____

_____

The Experience I want to have at work is (Secret 7) _____

_____

_____

_____

_____

_____

My preferred parameters are (Secret 2) _____

_____

_____

_____

_____

My transferrable skills (that I want to use!) are (Secret 2 & 3)

_____

_____

_____

_____

The awareness of your innate Career Design and Model of Success gives you the confidence to use this blueprint to find work that you love, while achieving more satisfaction. When you commit to only doing the work you were brought into this life to do, then real healing for yourself and others can begin to happen and healthy communities begin to form. Work is the ultimate source of community, and the place you spend the majority of your waking hours. Using these work hours wisely will heal you, and you will heal others through your work.

"Community is the spirit, the guiding light of the tribe, whereby people come together in order to fulfill a specific purpose, to help others fulfill their purpose, and to take care of one another. The goal of the community is to make sure that each member of the community is heard and is properly giving the gifts he has brought to the world. Without this giving, the community dies. And without the community, the

individual is left without a place where he can contribute. The
community is that grounding place where people come and share their
gifts and receive from others."
From "The Spirit of Intimacy, Ancient African Teachings in the
Way of Relationships"
Sobonfu Some

Too often, career transition is done in isolation and with a fair amount of shame. CWI believes that while we must look inside to discover our destiny and the answers to our personal questions, we still must look outside of ourselves to evolve to our greatest capacity. We need each other's design and care to grow into healthy humans and bring peace into our world. Work is medicine. Work is healing. Our hand is on your shoulder; our staff is here to support. Try to enjoy this journey to discovering your Inside Job. You will be changing the world in a most gentle and profound way, and no one will see it coming.

EPILOGUE

A Thank You Gift for Reading Our Book

How lovely you are—how unique and special. The value of rediscovering yourself and finding work that you can repeat over and over again is what we most hoped to teach you. We would like to conclude this book by reviewing The 8 Secrets to loving your work and thriving.

1. *Everything you know about career planning is backward.* Watch the myths you are operating under and ask yourself, "Is this my truth?" ("How does this feel in my body?")

2. *Remodeling your career.* To create your Inside Job, use the Model of Success to plan your next career move: Discover your Design; Explore the Experience you want to have; Decide the Parameters of your life, and select the Skills you want to use and want to develop.

3. *Jumping off the corporate ladder:* There is no linear model for success. Our careers are a series of cycles that are always "promoting" us through life. There are no mistakes, only lessons that hold value.

4. *Firing the 12-year-old running the show:* There are deeply ingrained, habituated thoughts that you created for yourself to explain the world you lived in before the age of 12. These

unconscious thoughts have caused neural pathways to form in your brain, and if you remain unaware of these thoughts/pathways, they will run your work-life. You will continue to select the same boss and co-workers and have the same experiences over and over again.

5. Don't *believe everything you think*: Except for your thinking, you are innately healthy. Understanding the three principles of the human experience guides you toward resilience, peace of mind, and an Inside Job.

6. *Staying in the eye of the storm*: Even when surrounded by utter chaos, you can make wise and calm decisions from a powerful mood. Your mood has everything to do with your job search, interviews, and relationships with others.

7. *Recalibrating your career goals*: To discover true career success, first focus on the experience you want to have, then plan your goals to achieve those experiences.

8. *The value of being yourself*: By uncovering and valuing your innate Career Design, you learn how to let yourself succeed. No matter what is happening with the economy, knowing your Career Design will make you resilient: You will be employable anywhere at any time, because you will not only know how to adapt your design to new and different work situations as needed, but you will find that new job opportunities will find you. Understanding your innate value is your Inside Job.

There are only two questions to ask yourself:

1. Are you ready to make your work an *Inside Job* and learn the 8 secrets to loving your work and thriving? And

2. Are you ready to discover—and do—the work you were designed to do in this lifetime?

If the answer is "Yes!," then we would like to offer you a gift. Please visit www.careerwisdominsitute.com and go to the Inside Job page to receive your free gift from the Career Wisdom Institute.

There are several ways you can work with the Career Wisdom Institute:

Inside Job: 8 Secrets to Loving Your Work and Thriving

We teach this course six times a year at our retreat offices in Moraga, California and through webinars. The Inside Job seminar is the required course for those who want to go into the six-week Master Series. The Inside Job Seminar reinforces all we have taught you in this book and gives you an opportunity to work directly with Julie and Sherry.

The Master Series

In the Master Series, our six-week program, you will: Identify and deepen your understanding of your Unique Design, harness your transferable skills, create your Career-Wise Resume, access the hidden job market, and prepare for and practice interviewing and salary negotiation. Upon the completion of the Master Series, you become part of the Career Wisdom Institute community and will receive free group mentoring twice monthly for one year from Julie and Sherry. The Master Series will be offered in our Moraga offices and through teleseminars.

Finally, Julie and Sherry are available for private consultations. We work in person, over the phone, and through Skype.

For more information, please visit our website, www.CareerWisdomInstitute.com.

MICHELE'S

Inspiring Story

Michele Franko,
Career Wisdom Institute Alumni Spring 2010

"Sometimes it is necessary to re-teach a thing its loveliness."
Galway Kinnell

When people say "it changed my life!" it's easy to think that whatever the miracle was that they were talking about would not apply to you, so I have always been a skeptic whenever I see that angle used in endorsements.

But in this case, I, in fact, did have my life changed by two angel guides who showed up for me when I most needed them. Sherry Berman, a personal referral, then joined by Julie Gleeson, appeared at a time when I was forced into a major life transition as I entered my 50s, without a college education and was emotionally devastated by a work/lifestyle lay-off from a horse breeding farm.

My career story began years ago when I was in humane law enforcement. Although I took an 8-year detour into the financial/corporate world I had dedicated 30 years of my life working with animals. My experience as a an animal cruelty investigator/humane officer years before always stayed with me and made me sensitive to the emotions and advocacy of animals, as well as the close bonds I made with them – so what to do?

Always having a scientific interest in animal behavior, I was keenly interested in social mammals, horses and elephants specifically. It was during my work with Sherry and Julie, that while perusing the bookstore, I noticed on the new releases table a book on elephant society and PTSD (Post Traumatic Stress Disorder) issues, and that set me on the path of an actual niche – trauma recovery and healing for animals. Everything I ever defended about all animals was there with the scientific research to back it up. I bought the book and brought it up in class with Sherry and Julie, and my assignment was to call the author and interview her. When I did, I was stunned that the author answered the phone herself, and that set everything in motion. That was late 2009, a couple of months after first meeting Sherry. During the next few months, the author and I developed a great relationship, and she referred me to the director of the Performing Animal Welfare Society, whom I had met while a humane officer when she started her first exotic animal sanctuary. Twenty-five years later, we met up again, and now I've now worked for her for two years as one of her senior elephant caregivers. In the meantime, I also work with the author and her organization, The Kerulos Center. It all made natural sense—what I discovered through Career Wisdom Institute were the things I do that I can't help doing: caring, healing, and bonding for/with non-human species, researching and advocacy—all on behalf of animals.

By putting myself totally into the work of the 8 Secrets and in the hands of the Career Wisdom Institute, I had several opportunities on the table within several months of my lay-off. The position I chose, elephant caregiver, which specifically is my path, was given to me without a real interview. Several pay increases later, I am doing well. Sherry and Julie helped me create my tag line – "My greatest honor is an animal at ease in my presence," and to this day, I keep our flow chart taped to the back of my office door, which I still refer to. The biggest comfort I have is that I know what my purpose is, and I can continue on my own path of peace and self-discovery.

What Career Wisdom Institute extracted from me were the underlying answers I had to my own questions about my purpose in life and destiny. Although they are not "therapists" in the definitive sense, they are natural masters who complement each other in bringing to light issues that have hindered your growth, your true gifts, drives, and what your experiences have taught you that you can in turn offer the world, and in doing so, give you the creativity, justification, and confidence to approach your life (professional and personal), with gusto and inspiration. By taking these approaches, you find yourself standing out to future peers, and as in my case, even making a bit of a name for yourself as you pursue your life/career. Sherry and Julie are prime examples of those using their true interests and gifts and sharing them with others as their own personal professions. What is so wonderful about them and why I'll always love them is that when working with you, you are the only thing that exists at that time. They are completely focused and absorbing everything you say and are determined to guide you to the answers you increasingly realize you are seeking, buried within you.

I don't know where I would be now, truly, if it weren't for Sherry, Julie, and Career Wisdom Institute. They have been the illuminating souls who finally led me down the yellow brick road.

Michele Franko, *Career Wisdom Institute Alumni*
Senior Elephant Caregiver, Performing Animal Welfare Society (PAWS); Senior Research Associate & Education Program Coordinator, The Kerulos Center

My greatest honor is an animal at ease in my presence...

Career Wisdom Institute Founders

JULIE GLEESON

Julie Gleeson brings over 20 years of experience as a consultant in the fields of stress elimination, couples mentoring, and collaborative team building to the Career Wisdom Institute. Her work guiding people to find their natural source of wisdom has helped clients find peace of mind, become more effective in their work and their lives, and achieve satisfaction, regardless of individual circumstances.

Julie's unique design is helping people understand that life is meant to be enjoyed and that each person already has exactly what he or she needs to feel fulfilled; as part of that design, she cannot help but hear the unique designs of her clients. She loves empowering people to see that there is nothing wrong with them, their partners, family members, coworkers, or their lives.

Julie's work is principle-based; that is, she teaches the principles that are central to the human experience. These human principles operate regardless of our understanding of them and help us deepen our power, resilience, and effectiveness.

In addition to her private consulting practice, over the years, Julie has worked inside corporations, owned retail stores (she was 18 when she bought her first store), and has done project management for workshops and programs. She is a past winner of the Peacemaker Award and volunteers her time in many eclectic areas, including as a former Court-Appointed Special Advocate, (supporting abused and neglected children) and as editor of the Norfolk Terrier National Magazine and email newsletter, all while actively raising and showing Norfolk Terriers.

SHERRY PLATT BERMAN

Sherry Platt Berman possesses 360-degrees of experience in the field of vocation identity, having worked as a hiring manager, recruiter, and career counselor over the last two decades. As a consultant for nonprofit organizations, high tech corporations, university career centers, and programs that serve the homeless, recovering drug addicts and alcoholics, as well as reformed convicts, Sherry has helped hundreds of people find work, regardless of their original circumstances.

Sherry draws from a variety of therapeutic foundations, including Buddhism, Western Psychology, Kabbalism, and Shamanic Traditions. She holds a Bachelor's degree in Communications from the University of Florida and a Master's in Counseling with a specialization in Life Transitions from the University of San Francisco.

She believes that it is no accident that the word "career" is primarily comprised of the word CARE. By co-founding the Career Wisdom Institute, Sherry helps people become happier and more satisfied in the workplace, which ultimately makes a real difference in the happiness and well-being of this world.

Suggested Reading List

PRINCIPLE-BASED LEARNING

The Missing Link, Reflections on Philosophy and Spirit
    Sydney Banks

The Quest of the Pearl
    Sydney Banks

The Enlightened Gardener
    Sydney Banks

The Enlightened Gardener Revisited
    Sydney Banks

Slowing Down to the Speed of Life
    Richard Carlson & J. Bailey

Don't Sweat the Small Stuff
    Richard Carlson, PhD

What About the Big Stuff?
    Richard Carlson, PhD

The Spark Inside (A Special Book for Youth)
    Ami Chen Mills-Naim

Customer Satisfaction Guaranteed
    Robert Kausen

We've GOT to Start Meeting Like This
    Robert Kausen

The Wisdom Within
    Roger Mills & Elsie

Spittle Wisdom for Life
    Elsie Spittle

The Relationship Handbook
  George S. Pransky, PhD

Modello, A Story of Hope for the Inner City and Beyond
  Jack Pransky

Parenting From the Heart
  Jack Pransky

TO DEEPEN YOUR PRACTICE

The Serenity Principle
  Joe Bailey

The Speed of Trust
  Stephen M. R. Covey

The Brain that Changes Itself
  Norman Doidge

Loving What Is, Four Questions That Can Change Your Life
  Byron Katie

A Thousand Names for Joy
  Byron Katie

Always We Begin Again, The Benedictine Way of Living
  John McQuiston

Brain Rules
  John Medina

The Fifth Discipline: The Art & Practice of the Learning Organization
  Peter Senge

SPIRITUAL GROWTH

Buddha's Brain
> Rick Hanson

There is Nothing Wrong with You
> Cheri Huber

Be the Person you Want to Find
> Cheri Huber

Getting Unstuck (CD)
> Pema Chodron

The Places that Scare You: A Guide to Fearlessness in Difficult Times
> Pema Chodron

The Miracle of Mindfulness
> Thich Nhat Hanh

The Prophet
> Kahlil Gibran

Siddhartha
> Hermann Hesse

The Journey Home: A Kryon Parable, The Story of Michael Thomas and the Seven Angels
> Lee Carroll

The Spiral Dance
> Starhawk

Undefended Love
> Marlena S. Lyons

The Highly Sensitive Person
> Elaine N. Aron Ph.D.

The Only Diet There Is
> Sondra Ray

SWAMI MUKTANANDA

Meditate
I have become Alive

SWAMI CHIDVILASANANDA

Enthusiasm; The Yoga of Discipline
Gurumayi

PROFESSIONAL

Women Don't Ask: Negotiation and the Gender Divide
Linda Babcock

The Female Brain
Louann Brizendine M.D

Enlightened Power: How Women are Transforming the Practice of Leadership
Lin Coughlin

If You've Raised Kids, You Can Manage Anything: Leadership Begins At Home
Ann Crittenden

The Price of Motherhood: Why the Most Important Job in the World is Still the Least Valued
Ann Crittenden

The New Feminine Brain: Developing Your Intuitive Genius
Mona Lisa Schulz

Made in the USA
Charleston, SC
30 July 2013